SNAPSHOT

Lisbon

CONTENTS

Post-Pandemic Travels: Expect a Warm Welcome...and a Few Changes
Research for this guidebook was limited by the COVID-19 outbreak, and the long-term impact of the crisis on our recommended destinations is unclear. Some details in this book will change for post-pandemic travelers. Now more than ever, it's smart to reconfirm specifics as you plan and travel. As always, you can find major updates at RickSteves.com/update.

SIGHTS

1. Aljube Museum of Resistance & Freedom
2. To Bullring
3. Cathedral (Sé)
4. "Eating Lane"
5. Fado Museum
6. To Gulbenkian Museum
7. Mercado da Ribeira
8. Museum & School of Portuguese Decorative Arts
9. To Museum of Ancient Art
10. National Theater
11. To National Tile Museum & Parque das Nações
12. Praça do Comércio
13. Praça dos Restauradores
14. Rossio
15. São Jorge Castle

Walks

16. Start of Alfama Stroll
17. Start of Baixa Stroll
18. Start of Bairro Alto & Chiado Stroll

Funiculars & Viewpoints

19. Elevador da Bica
20. Elevador da Glória
21. Elevador de Santa Justa
22. Miradouro das Portas do Sol
23. Miradouro de Santa Luzia
24. Miradouro de São Jorge
25. Miradouro de São Pedro de Alcântara

Funicular
Pedestrian-Friendly Area
Popular Shopping Area
Self-Guided Walking Tours

Baixa Stroll

ELEVATOR DA GLÓRIA
OBELISK
Praça dos Restauradores
WALK ENDS
ROSSIO TRAIN STATION
CALÇADA WORKER MEMORIAL
NAT'L THEATER
ABEP TICKET KIOSK
Largo de São Domingos
SÃO DOMINGOS
Praça da Figueira
SWEETS
CONVENTO DO CARMO
ELEVADOR STA. JUSTA
BAIXA
Rossio (Praça Dom Pedro IV)
ROSSIO
Largo do Cadoval
Largo do Carmo
CHIADO
ARMAZÉNS DO CHIADO MALL
Baixa-Chiado
ARCH
ELEVATOR UP TO SÃO JORGE CASTLE
To Alfama
"HIDDEN CHURCH"
MUDE
MARTINHO DA ARCADA CAFÉ
ARCH OF TRIUMPH
LISBON WALKER
Praça do Comércio
Praça do Município
WALK BEGINS
WINE-TASTING CENTER
Terreiro do Paço
PILLARS
Rio Tejo

Street/place labels: AV. DA CONDES, COLISEU, To Elevador do Lavra, R. PORTAS S. ANTÃO, S. ANT., R. REGEDOR, QUERIOZ, CAL. NOVA, RUA DE PALMA, R. ARCO D. GRAÇA, #12E & 20E, Praça Martim Moniz, Martim Moniz, RUA DE MOURARIA, Rossio, Bus Tours, #714, #12E & 15E, R. BORRATEM, To Alfama, R. BESTEGA, R. DA VITORIA, RUA SANTA JUSTA, RUA DA PRATA, RUA DOS DOURADORES, RUA DOS FANQUEIROS, RUA DA MADALENA, RUA DA ASSUNÇÃO, RUA AUGUSTA, R. DOS CORREEIROS, S. NICOLAU, To Alfama, R. DE CONCEIÇÃO, #28E, RUA DE COMÉRCIO, RUA DE SÃO JULIÃO, C. S. FRANCISCO, RUA DO COMÉRCIO, #15E, #28E, AV. RIBEIRA DAS NAUS, To Cais do Sodré Station via Riverside Promenade, R. C. DUQUE, R. DO DUQUE, R. DA OLIVIERA, RUA NOVA TRINDADE, R. DA TRINDADE, TR. DO CARMO, RUA GARRETT, To Bairro Alto, RUA CARDOSO, SERPA PINTO, Baixa-Chiado, R. S. FRAN., R. DO CRUCIFIXO, RUA DOS SAPATEIROS, RUA AUREA, R. DO OURO, R. S. FRANCISCO, R. CAPELO, Baixa-Chiado, R. CONDESA

- **1** Praça do Comércio
- **2** Lisbon's Riverfront
- **3** Rua do Comércio
- **4** Rua de São Julião
- **5** Church of St. Nicholas
- **6** Praça da Figueira
- **7** Church of São Domingos
- **8** Largo de São Domingos
- **9** Ginjinha Bars (2)
- **10** Rossio Square
- **11** Rossio Station
- **12** Praça dos Restauradores
- **13** To Avenida da Liberdade & Pombal Statue

N

200 Meters
200 Yards

Bairro Alto & Chiado Stroll

R. DA GLÓRIA
R. ST. GLÓRIA
RUA TAIPAS
AVENIDA DA LIBERDADE
R. DA SÃO JOSÉ
CONDES
To Elevador do Lavra
COLISEU
S. ANT.

WALK BEGINS

ELEVADOR DA GLÓRIA

R. DOM PEDRO V
R. S. PEDRO DE ALCÂNTARA

São Pedro de Alcântara Park

RUA COELHO

TR. S. PEDRO
TR. R. MOUROS
R. TEIXEIRA

OBELISK

Praça dos Restauradores

Restauradores
CALÇADA WORKERS MEMORIAL
ABEP TICKET KIOSK
NAT'L THEATER
Largo de São Domingos

R. PORTAS S'ANTÃO
REGEDOR

ROSSIO TRAIN STATION

ROSSIO

Rossio (Praça Dom Pedro IV)

SOLAR DO VINHO DO PORTO

TR. BOA HORA

IGREJA SÃO ROQUE

❶

C. DA GLÓRIA

❷

R. AGUA FLOR

RUA DA ROSA
RUA DA ATALAIA

R. DO GRÉMIO

T.D. QUEIMADA

❸ MUSEU DE ARTE SACRA

R. MISERICÓRDIA

Largo Trindade Coelho

RUA C. DUQUE
R. DO DUQUE
R. DA CONDESA
R. DA OLIVEIRA

Largo do Cadoval

BAIXA

RUA 1 DEZEMBRO
RUA ÁUREA
ARCH

BAIRRO ALTO

R. LUZ SORIANO
RUA DA ROSA
R. BARROCA
RUA GAVEAS
NOTICIAS
RUA NOVA TRINDADE

T. DOS FIEIS DE DEUS
TV. ESPERA
TR. MERCES
R. DO NORTE

To Miradouro de Santa Catarina

❹

BAIRRO DO AVILLEZ

MUSIC SHOP

CONVENTO DO CARMO ❻

ELEVADOR STA. JUSTA ❼

TEATRO DA TRINDADE

R. DA TRINDADE

Largo do Carmo ❺

TR. DO CARMO

R. DO CARMO
R. DO OURO

WALK ENDS

TR. TRIN

CHIADO

R. CAL. R. LORETO
Praça Luís de Camões
#28E

ELEVADOR DA BICA

R. D. CHAGAS

RUA H. SECA

R.ST. CAT. T.G. COUSSUL

BICA

FLORES
RUA DO ALECRIM
R. ATAÍDE

#28E

❽ Largo Chiado
Baixa-Chiado

❾ RUA GARRETT

A VIDA PORTUGUESA

ARMAZÉNS DO CHIADO MALL
Baixa-Chiado

RUA S. FRAN.
RUA IVENS

R. SERPA PINTO

SÃO CARLOS THEATER

R. CAPELO

RUA A. MARIA CARDOSO
RUA D. DE BRAGANÇA

BIBLIOTECA PÚBLICA

Largo da Pública

To Baixa & Alfama

C. SAN FRANCISCO

200 Meters

200 Yards

RUA VITOR CÓRDON
#28E

Praça do Município

❶ Miradouro de São Pedro de Alcântara
❷ Bairro Alto Detour
❸ São Roque Church
❹ Cervejaria da Trindade
❺ Largo do Carmo
❻ Convento do Carmo
❼ Elevador de Santa Justa
❽ Café A Brasileira
❾ Rua Garrett

INTRODUCTION

This Snapshot guide, excerpted from my guidebook *Rick Steves Portugal*, introduces you to Lisbon, the country's culturally rich capital. Here at the far western edge of Europe, prices are reasonable, the people are warm, and the pace of life slows. Lisbon's neighborhoods—dotted with museums, inviting eateries, and squares grand and small—are connected by historic trolleys and mosaic sidewalks. Wander through the city's characteristic downtown neighborhoods like the hilly Alfama, the exotic Mouraria, and the busy Baixa, then head up to the lanes of Bairro Alto at night to find a good fado bar. The grand Belém district offers a look at Lisbon's historic architecture and seafaring glory, from the 16th-century Monastery of Jerónimos to the Monument to the Discoveries. Or visit the Gulbenkian Museum, the best of Lisbon's 40 museums, offering 5,000 years' worth of art.

Day-trip to the touristy but lovely town of Sintra, a former aristocratic retreat that's dotted with sights such as the fanciful Pena Palace, royal National Palace, and evocative Moorish castle ruins atop a hill.

To help you have the best trip possible, I've included the following topics in this book:

• **Planning Your Time,** with advice on how to make the most of your limited time

• **Orientation,** including tourist information offices (abbreviated as TI), tips on public transportation, local tour options, and helpful hints

• **Sights,** with ratings and strategies for meaningful and efficient visits

• **Sleeping and Eating,** with good-value recommendations in every price range

• **Connections,** with tips on trains, buses, and driving

Practicalities, near the end of this book, has information on money, staying connected, hotel reservations, transportation, and other useful tips, plus Portuguese survival phrases.

To travel smartly, read this little book in its entirety before you go. It's my hope that this guide will make your trip more meaningful and rewarding. Traveling like a temporary local, you'll get the absolute most out of every mile, minute, and dollar.

Boa viagem! Happy travels!

Rick Steves

LISBON

Lisboa

Lisbon is ramshackle, trendy, and charming all at once—an endearing mix of now and then. Vintage trolleys shiver up and down its hills, bird-stained statues mark grand squares, taxis rattle and screech through cobbled lanes, and Art Nouveau cafés are filled equally with well-worn and well-dressed locals—nursing their coffees side-by-side. It's a city of proud ironwork balconies, multicolored tiles, and mosaic sidewalks; of bougainvillea and red-tiled roofs with antique TV antennas; and of foodie haunts and designer boutiques.

Lisbon, Portugal's capital, is the country's banking and manufacturing center. Residents call their city Lisboa (leezh-BOH-ah), which comes from the Phoenician *Alis Ubbo*, meaning "calm port." A port city on the yawning mouth of the Rio Tejo (REE-oo TAY-zhoo—the Tagus River), Lisbon welcomes large ships to its waters and state-of-the-art dry docks. And more recently, it has become a hugely popular stop with cruise ships.

Romans (2nd century BC) and Moors (8th century) were the earliest settlers in Lisbon, but the city's glory days were in the 15th and 16th centuries, when explorers such as Vasco da Gama opened new trade routes around Africa to India, making Lisbon one of Europe's richest cities. Portugal's Age of Discovery fueled rapid economic growth, which sparked the flamboyant art boom called the Manueline period—named for King Manuel I (r. 1495-1521).

On the morning of All Saints' Day in 1755, a tremendous off-shore earthquake rocked Lisbon, followed by a devastating tsunami and days of fires. Chief Minister Marquês de Pombal rebuilt downtown Lisbon on a grid plan, with broad boulevards and generous squares. It's this "Pombaline"-era neighborhood where you'll spend

LISBON

much of your time, though remnants of Lisbon's pre-earthquake charm survive in Belém, the Alfama, and the Bairro Alto district. The bulk of your sightseeing will likely be in these neighborhoods.

As the Paris of the Portuguese-speaking world, Lisbon (pop. 548,000 in the core) is the Old World capital of its former empire, which once had some 100 million people and stretched from Europe to Brazil, and Africa to China. Portugal remains on largely good terms with its former colonies—and immigrants from places such as Mozambique and Angola add diversity and flavor to the city; it's likely that you'll hear African music as much as Portuguese fado.

With its characteristic hills, trolleys, famous suspension bridge, and rolling fog, Lisbon has a San Francisco feel. Enjoy all that this world-class city has to offer: elegant outdoor cafés, exciting art, fun-to-browse shops, stunning vistas, delicious food, entertaining museums, and a salty sailors' quarter with a hill-capping castle.

PLANNING YOUR TIME

Lisbon merits at least three days, including a day for a side-trip to Sintra. If you have more time, there's plenty to do.

Day 1

Get oriented to Lisbon's three downtown neighborhoods (following my three self-guided walks): Alfama, Baixa, and Bairro Alto/Chiado. Start where the city did, at its castle (hop a taxi or Uber to get there at 9:00, before the crowds hit). After surveying the city from the highest viewpoint in town, walk downhill into the characteristic Alfama neighborhood and end at the Fado Museum. From there, zip over to the big main square (Praça do Comércio) to explore the Baixa, then ride up the Elevador da Glória funicular (or taxi) to begin the Bairro Alto and Chiado walk. Art lovers can then hop the Metro or a taxi to the Gulbenkian Museum (open until 18:00, closed Tue), while shoppers can browse the boutiques of the Chiado neighborhood and Príncipe Real. Consider dinner at a fado show in the Bairro Alto or the Alfama. For more evening options, see "Entertainment in Lisbon," later.

Day 2

Trolley to Belém and tour the monastery, tower, and National Coach Museum. Have lunch in Belém, then tour the Museum of Ancient Art on your way back to Lisbon.

Day 3

Side-trip to Sintra to tour the Pena Palace and explore the ruined Moorish castle.

More Time

With extra days, slow down and relax—spreading the "Day 1" activities over two days. Or use the time to explore and window-shop characteristic neighborhoods and nurse drinks bought from kiosks on relaxing squares. You could also head to the Parque das Nações or take a food tour.

Monday Options

Many top sights are closed on Monday, particularly in Belém. That'd be a good day to visit the Gulbenkian Museum, take my self-guided neighborhood walks, day-trip to Sintra, go on a guided walking tour (see "Tours in Lisbon," later), or head to Parque das Nações for a dose of modern Lisbon.

Orientation to Lisbon

LISBON: A VERBAL MAP

Greater Lisbon has close to three million people and intimidating sprawl. Most visitors spend virtually all their time in the old city

Lisbon Center

To Intendente

R. DAM. MONTEIRO

R. DE SÃO LAZARO

RUA DE BENFORMOSO

R. D. OLARIAS

C. DO MONTE

T #28E

CONVENTO
N. S. DA
GRAÇA

Largo
da
Graça

RUA DA R. ROSALINA

RUA DO BENFORMOSO

R. TERREIRINHO

R. DOS CAVALEIROS

**Praça
Martim Moniz
("Dragon Square")**

T #12E
& 28E

RUA DA PALMA

RUA DO OULEIRO

RUA CAPELÃO

**Largo do
Terreirinho**

T #12E

M
Martim
Moniz

RUA M. P. DE LIMA

RUA DE MOURARIA

MOURARIA

P. DE COLEGINHO

C. DE SANTO ANDRÉ

C. DE GRAÇA

C. DAS MONICAS

RUA V. DO OPERARIO

DE SÃO VICENTE

C. DE SÃO VICENTE

SÃO VICENTE
DE FORA
MONASTERY

COSTA DO CASTELO

TELHEIRO

**CASTELO DE
SÃO JORGE**

SANTA
CRUZ

R. MEN. DEUS

R. SÃO TOMÉ

T #12E

R. DE S. GRIND

R. ESCOLAS GERAIS

T #28E

R. D. SALVADOR

**CASTLE
TOWN**

MENINO
DEUS

**Largo
Portas
do Sol**

T
#12E &
28E

T #28E

R. ESCOLAS

**DEC. ARTS
MUSEUM**

**SÃO
ESTÊVÃO**

S. CRISTÓVÃO

C.M. TANCOS

T #12E

MARKET

ELEV.
#2

CHÃO DA FEIRA

R. DO C. MOR.

**WALKING
ROUTE TO
CASTLE**

S. HELENA

R. DE S. MIGUEL

RUA REGUEIRA

S. MARÇAL

**Largo da
Costa**

**ELEVATOR
#1**

RUA DOS FANQUEIROS

RUA DA MADALENA

R. DE SÃO MAMEDE

RUA M. S. ANTONIO

L. LOIOS

S. TIAGO

R. SAÚDE

**Largo
Santa
Luzia**

R. AGUAIO

T
#12E &
28E

**S.
MIGUEL**

S. PEDRO

**Largo Chafariz
de Dentro**

**FADO
MUSEUM**

R.P. NEGRAS

CONCEIÇÃO

R. DOURADORES

T #12E
16E & 2BE

R. S. ANT.

S.
ANTONIO

CRUZES DA SÉ

**ALJUBE
MUSEUM**

T
#12E &
28E

R. D. LIMOEIRO

ALFAMA

R. JUDIARIA

To
Santa
Apolónia
& Oriente
Train Stations

R. PADARIA

**CATHEDRAL
(SÉ)**

RUA S. J. DA PRAÇA

R. D. TERREIRO TRIGO

R. BACALHOEIROS

R. D. CAIS D. SANTAREM

**Doca do
Terreiro
do Trigo**

RUA DA ALFÂNDEGA

#15E
T

**Campo
das
Cebolas**

INFANTE DOM HENRIQUE

AVENIDA

**Praça
do
Comércio**

Terreiro do
M Paço

Terreiro do
M Paço

Doca da Marina

PILLARS

RIVER
CRUISES

**TERREIRO DO PAÇO
FERRY TERMINAL**

RIO

Rio Tejo

To Barreiro &
Montijo

200 Meters

200 Yards

center, a delightful series of parks, boulevards, and squares in a crusty, well-preserved architectural shell. But even on a brief visit, you'll also want to venture to Belém, the riverfront suburb with many top sights.

Here's an overview of the city's layout:

Baixa (Lower Town): Downtown Lisbon fills a valley flanked by two hills along the banks of the Rio Tejo. In that valley, the neighborhood called Baixa (BYE-shah) stretches from the main squares—Rossio (roh-SEE-oo) and Praça da Figueira (PRAH-sah dah fee-GAY-rah)—to the waterfront. The Baixa is a flat, pleasant shopping area of grid-patterned streets. As Lisbon's main crossroads and transportation hub, touristy Baixa has lots of hotels, venerable cafés and pastry shops, and kitschy souvenir stands.

Alfama: The hill to the east of the Baixa is the Alfama (al-FAH-mah), a colorful tangle of medieval streets, topped by São Jorge Castle. The lower slopes of the Alfama are a spilled spaghetti of old sailors' homes.

Mouraria: The old Muslim Quarter and the birthplace of fado, this district (next to the Alfama, between the castle and Praça Martim Moniz) is now the center of Lisbon's international community and emerging as a fun and trendy place to explore.

Bairro Alto (High Town): The hill to the west of the Baixa is capped by the Bairro Alto (BYE-roh AHL-too), with a tight grid of steep, narrow, and characteristic lanes. Downhill toward the Baixa, the Bairro Alto fades into the trendy and inviting **Chiado** (shee-AH-doo), with linger-a-while squares, upmarket restaurants, and high-fashion stores.

Modern Lisbon: From the historic core, the modern city stretches north (sloping uphill) along wide Avenida da Liberdade and beyond (way beyond), where you find Edward VII Park, the Gulbenkian Museum, breezy botanical gardens, the bullring, and the airport.

Away from the Center: Along the riverfront are several worthwhile areas. Three miles west of the center is the suburb of **Belém** (beh-LAYNG), home to much of Lisbon's best sightseeing, with several Age of Discovery sights (particularly the Monastery of Jerónimos)—and you can visit the Museum of Ancient Art along the way. Five miles north of the center is **Parque das Nações,** site of the Expo '98 world's fair and now a modern shopping complex and riverfront promenade (the National Tile Museum is about halfway there). And across the Rio Tejo, **Cacilhas** (kah-SEE-la-hsh) is a tiny and characteristic little port that few tourists visit (an easy ferry ride from the center; from there you can bus or taxi to the towering Cristo Rei statue).

TOURIST INFORMATION

Lisbon has several tourist offices—all branded "ask me Lisboa"—and additional information kiosks sprout around town during the busy summer months (www.visitlisboa.com). The main city TIs have the same hours (daily 9:00-20:00) and are located on **Praça dos Restauradores** at Palácio Foz (+351 213 463 314; national TI in same office; there's also a kiosk across the street) and on Praça do Comércio (two locations; +351 210 312 810). Another TI is at the airport (daily 7:00-24:00, +351 218 450 660).

Smaller TI kiosks are at the bottom of **Rossio**; across the street from the monastery in **Belém**; at **Parque das Nações**, at the riverfront side of the **Vasco da Gama mall;** and inside **Santa Apolónia train station** (end of track 3). At any TI, you can buy a LisboaCard (see next) and pick up the free city map and information-packed *Follow Me Lisboa* booklet (monthly, cultural and museum listings—also available at www.visitlisboa.com, "Publications" tab).

LisboaCard: This card covers all public transportation (including trains to Sintra and Cascais) and free entry to many museums (including the Museum of Ancient Art, National Tile Museum, National Coach Museum, Monastery of Jerónimos, and Belém Tower). It also provides discounts on river cruises, my two recommended city tours, and many museums (including sights at Sintra). You can buy the card at Lisbon's TIs (including the airport TI), but not at participating sights. If you plan to museum-hop, the card is a good value, particularly for a day in Belém, though it does not allow you to skip lines at busy monuments (like those in Belém). The card is unnecessary if you're a student or senior, for whom most sights are free or half-price. Carry the LisboaCard booklet with you—some discounts require coupons contained inside (€20/24 hours, €34/48 hours, €42/72 hours, kids 5-11 nearly half-price, includes excellent explanatory guidebook, www.visitlisboa.com). Remember that many sights are closed on Monday—it's best to buy the card when you can use it for consecutive days.

ARRIVAL IN LISBON

For complete information on arriving at or departing from Lisbon by plane, train, bus, and cruise ship, see "Lisbon Connections" at the end of this chapter.

By Plane: International and domestic flights arrive at Lisbon's Portela Airport. On arrival, check in at the handy TI—it's a smart place to buy your LisboaCard. Options for getting into town include taxis, Uber, Aerobus, or Metro (all described later).

By Train: Lisbon has four primary train stations: Santa Apolónia (Spain and most points north), Oriente (Algarve, Évora, Sintra, and fast trains to the north), Rossio (Sintra, Óbidos, and Nazaré), and Cais do Sodré (coastal Belém, Estoril, and Cascais). For schedules, see www.cp.pt.

By Car: It makes absolutely no sense to drive in Lisbon. Dump your rental car at the airport and connect to your hotel by taxi or Uber (car return clearly marked; the airport is also a good place to pick up a car on your way out of town).

If you must drive and are entering Lisbon from the north, a series of boulevards takes you into the center. Navigate by following signs to *Centro, Avenida da República, Marquês de Pombal, Avenida da Liberdade, Praça dos Restauradores, Rossio,* and *Praça do Comércio*. If coming from the east over the Vasco da Gama Bridge and heading for the airport, just follow the signs. There are many safe underground pay **parking** lots in Lisbon (follow blue *P* signs; the most central is at Praça dos Restauradores), but they discourage longer stays by getting more expensive by the hour. Expect to pay over €20/day.

HELPFUL HINTS

Free Days and Monday Closures: The Gulbenkian Museum is free every Sunday after 14:00 (and one of the few museums open on Monday). Many major sights are closed on Monday, including Lisbon's Museum of Ancient Art, National Tile Museum, and Fado Museum, as well as Belém's Monastery of Jerónimos, Coach Museum, and Belém Tower.

Theft Alert: Lisbon has piles of people doing illegal business on the street. Enjoy the sightseeing, but wear your money belt and keep your pack zipped up. Pickpockets target tourists at popular sights and on trolleys, elevators, and funiculars. Some thieves pose as tourists by wearing cameras and toting maps. Be on guard whenever you're in a crush of people or jostled as you enter or leave a tram or bus. Beggars are often pickpockets. Teams of pickpockets create confusion and congestion.

Violence is very rare, and you'll see lots of police stationed throughout town. While the city is generally safe, if you're looking for trouble—especially after dark—you may find it.

Market Days: Tuesdays and Saturdays are flea- and food-market days in the Alfama's Campo de Santa Clara. On Sundays, the LX Factory zone, in the shadow of the 25th of April Bridge, hosts a lively farmers market (9:30-16:00; for location, see the "Lisbon Overview" map, earlier).

Pedestrian Warnings: Lisbon's unique black-and-white patterned tile pavement, while picturesque, can be very slippery. And trams can be quiet and sneak up on you if you're not paying attention. Even some of the tuk-tuks are "eco" (electric) and can zip up behind you silently.

Laundry: Centrally located **5àSec Lavandaria** can usually provide same-day service if you drop off early (Mon-Fri 8:00-20:00, Sat from 10:00, closed Sun, next to the bottom level of the Armazéns do Chiado mall and lower entry to the Baixa-Chiado Metro stop at Rua do Crucifixo 99, +351 213 479 599). **WashStation Baixa-Castelo** is a small self-service launderette just up from Praça da Figueira (daily 8:00-22:00, Rua da Madalena 231, mobile +351 919 772 701). For locations, see the "Lisbon Center Hotels" map on page 108.

Travel Agency: GeoStar is helpful for train tickets (Portugal only) and flights (Mon-Fri 9:00-18:30, closed Sat-Sun, Praça Duque da Terceira 1, near the Cais do Sodré station, +351 213 405 380).

Ticket Kiosk: The green **ABEP kiosk** at the bottom end of Praça dos Restauradores is a handy spot to buy a city transit pass, LisboaCard, and tickets to bullfights, soccer games, concerts, and other events (daily 9:00-20:00).

GETTING AROUND LISBON
By Public Transit

Lisbon is easy—even fun—to navigate by Metro, funicular, trolley, and bus. And one transit card covers them all.

Tickets

If you have a **LisboaCard** (see "Tourist Information," earlier), you can use it to ride Lisbon's public transit. Otherwise, buy a Viva Viagem card, which works on the Metro, funiculars, trolleys, buses, Santa Justa elevator, ferry to Cacilhas, and some short-distance trains (on some transit you can buy tickets from the driver, but that's more expensive). For transit information, see www.carris.pt.

Viva Viagem Card: Transit tickets are issued on the scannable, reloadable Viva Viagem card (€0.50 for the card itself, not shareable—each rider needs one). You can buy or reload the card at ticket windows or machines in Metro stations (touch "without a reusable card" for first-time users, or "with a reusable card" to top up; bright yellow machines accept only credit cards). Keep your Viva Viagem card handy—you'll need to place it on the magnetic pad when entering and leaving the system.

You can use the Viva Viagem in three ways:

A **single-ride ticket** costs €1.50 (good for one hour of travel within Zone 1). But if you're taking even a few rides, "zapping" is a much better deal (see later).

A **24-hour pass** costs €6.40 (this version does not cover trains). If taking five or more rides in a day, this is the best deal. If you're side-tripping to Sintra or Cascais, consider the €10.60 version, which includes trains to those towns (but not the bus at Sintra). Skip the €9.55 version of the 24-hour pass, which adds the ferry to Cacilhas (it's cheaper to buy that separately).

"Zapping" lets you preload the card with anywhere from €3 to €40 and lowers the per-ride cost to €1.35 for all forms of transit. Figure out how much you'll need and load it up (estimate conservatively—you can always top up later, but leftover credit is nonrefundable). Unlike the 24-hour pass, zapping can be used for trains to Sintra and Cascais.

Without Viva Viagem: Although it's possible to **pay the driver** as you board buses (€2), trolleys (€3—more than double the Viva Viagem price), funiculars (€3.80 for two trips), and the Santa Justa elevator (€5.30), only suckers do that. It's much cheaper if you get comfortable zapping with Viva Viagem.

Metro

Lisbon's simple, fast, and color-coded subway system is a delight to use (runs daily 6:30-1:00 in the morning). Though it's not necessary for getting around the historic downtown, the Metro is handy for trips to or from Rossio (M: Rossio or Restauradores), Praça do Comércio (M: Terreiro do Paço), the Gulbenkian Museum (M: São Sebastião), the Chiado neighborhood (M: Baixa-Chiado), Parque das Nações and the Oriente train sta-

tion (both at M: Oriente), Sete Rios bus and train stations (M: Jardim Zoológico), and the airport (M: Aeroporto). Metro stops are marked above ground with a red "M." *Saída* means "exit." You can find a Metro map at any Metro stop, on most city maps, and at www.metrolisboa.pt.

Sightseeing by Metro: To make your sightseeing commutes quicker and easier, link together sights on the same Metro line. For example, Praça do Comércio, Rossio, and the Gulbenkian Museum can be laced together by Metro faster than via taxi. You can even sightsee as you travel: All Metro stations have wonderful, museum-worthy tile panels. The blue line between Parque and Colégio Militar/Luz has some of the best art; with a 24-hour transit pass, you can hop on and off and explore as many stations as you like.

Buses and Trolleys

Buses and trolleys usually share the same stops and routes. Signs for bus stops list the bus number, while signs for trolley stops in-

clude an E (for *eléctrico*) before or after the route number. Though Lisbon's buses are fine, for fun and practical public transportation, ride the trolleys (and funiculars—see later).

Like San Francisco, Lisbon sees its classic trolleys as part of its heritage, and has kept a few in use: Trolleys #12E (circling

the Alfama), #24E (to Campolide), and #28E (a scenic ride across the old town) use vintage cars; #15E (to Belém) uses a modern, air-conditioned version. Make sure you have a ticket or pass and that you validate your Viva Viagem card as you enter...or risk a big fine on the spot. Trolleys rattle by every 10 minutes or so (every 15-20 minutes after 19:00) and run until about 23:00. Most pickpocketing in Lisbon takes place on trolleys, so enjoy the ride, but keep an eye on your belongings.

While lines #28E and #12E seem made-to-order for tourist use, they are often unbearably crowded. If you can deal with the often-overwhelming crowds (see the tips, next), these trolleys can work as hop-on, hop-off do-it-yourself tours. For a stop-by-stop rundown, see "Touring Lisbon by Trolley" in the next section.

Crowd-Beating Tips: Lisbon's trolleys are an absolute joy...*if* you're sitting down and looking out the window with the wind in your face. But if you have to stand, you won't be able to see out the (low) windows, and you'll spend the jostling ride trying to steady yourself. At peak times, hordes of tourists wait at trolley stops (particularly at starting points) and pickpockets abound. To enjoy a trolley with fewer crowd frustrations, consider these strategies:

1. Rather than being determined to take a particular trolley at a particular time, keep an eye on trolleys as they roll by. If an empty trolley pulls up, hop on and take advantage of the open space.

2. Consider waking early and making a trolley ride your first experience of the day. Trolleys "open" before any museums, so if you arrive in the early morning you can beat the tourist crush, get a seat, and see the city wake up. Late departures (after dinner) also have fewer crowds.

3. Ride line #24E, which runs a less-touristy route and can be less crowded.

4. Take a private trolley tour (see "Tours in Lisbon," later).

5. If you'll be going to Porto, wait to enjoy a vintage trolley

LISBON

there: Porto's trolleys are just as memorable as Lisbon's and have no crowds.

Funiculars

Lisbon's funiculars include the Elevador da Glória (linking Avenida da Liberdade to the Bairro Alto) and the Elevador da Bica (rising from Rua de São Paulo, near the river, to the Bairro Alto). Funiculars depart about every 10 minutes.

By Taxi or Uber

Lisbon is a great **taxi** town. Especially if you're with a companion, Lisbon's cabs are a cheap time-saver; groups of three or four should taxi everywhere. Rides start at €4, and you can go anywhere in the center for around €6. Window decals clearly spell out all charges in English. Be sure your driver turns on the meter; it should start at about €4 and be set to *Tarifa 1* (Mon-Fri 6:00-21:00, including the airport) or *Tarifa 2* (same drop rate, a little more per kilometer; for nights, weekends, and holidays). If the meter reads *Tarifa 3, 4,* or *5,* simply ask the cabbie to change it, unless you're going to Belém, which is considered outside the city limits.

Cabs are generally easy to hail on the street (green light means available, lit number on the roof indicates it's taken). If you're having a hard time flagging one down, it's likely because you're standing near but not quite at a taxi stand. Ask a passerby for the location of the nearest taxi stand: *praça de taxi* (PRAH-sah duh taxi). They're all over the town center.

Lisbon is also an excellent **Uber** town. The ride-sharing app works here just like back home; it's at least as affordable as a taxi (often cheaper, except during "surge" pricing); and the drivers and their cars are generally of great quality. If you've never tried Uber abroad, do it here. Sit in front and talk!

Tours in Lisbon

ON WHEELS
▲▲Touring Lisbon by Trolley

Lisbon's trolleys—many of them vintage models from the 1920s—shake and shiver through the old parts of town, somehow safely weaving within inches of parked cars, climbing steep hills, and offering sightseers breezy views (rubberneck out the window and you die). You can use the following trolley lines as an inexpensive way to tour the city. As you board, swipe your Viva Viagem card or pay the driver, and take a seat (zapping tickets are good for an hour, and a 24-hour pass comes with unlimited hopping on and off).

Be aware that lines #28E and #12E are jam-packed with tourists and often come with ridiculous lines. Trolley #24E runs away

Lisbon's Best Viewpoints

The first three viewpoints are included in the self-guided walks described in this chapter:

- Miradouro de São Pedro de Alcântara (view terrace in Bairro Alto, at top of Elevador da Glória funicular; see the "Bairro Alto and Chiado Stroll," later)
- São Jorge Castle (on top of the Alfama; see photo above and the "Alfama Stroll and the Castle," later)
- Miradouro das Portas do Sol (south slope of Alfama; see the "Alfama Stroll and the Castle," later)
- Elevador de Santa Justa (in the Baixa, page 52)
- Cristo Rei (statue on hillside across the Rio Tejo, page 90)
- Edward VII Park (at north end of Avenida da Liberdade)
- Miradouro de Santa Catarina (near the top of the Elevador da Bica funicular)
- Miradouro da Graça and Miradouro da Senhora do Monte (same neighborhood overlooking the São Jorge Castle)

from the central tourist zone and can be less crowded. For tips on riding the trolley, including avoiding crowds, see "Getting Around Lisbon," earlier.

Trolley #28E

Trolley #28E is a San Francisco-style Lisbon joyride (runs about 5:45-22:30; after 21:15, service is limited to stops between Estrela and Graça). The following are notable stops from west to east:

Campo Ourique: The **Prazeres Cemetery,** at the western terminus of route #28E, is a vast park-like necropolis with good bridge views, dense with the mausoleums of leading Lisbon families and historic figures dating back to the 19th century (daily 9:00-17:00).

Igreja Sto. Condestável: The first stop after the cemetery is next to an angular modern church. Hiding just behind the church is the **Mercado de Campo de Ourique,** a 19th-century iron-and-glass market that's now a trendy food circus (see page 121).

Estrela: Two stops later, the trolley pulls up in front of another large church (on the right). The 18th-century, late Baroque **Estrela Basilica** has stairs winding up to the roof for a view both out and down into the church (€4, daily 10:00-18:00). Across the street is the gate into **Estrela Park,** a cozy neighborhood scene with exotic plants, a pond-side café, and a playground.

Assembleia da República: At the next stop, you'll see a garden poking up on the left behind a high wall (which hides the prime minister's residence). Next up is the huge, stately Assembly of the Republic building—home to Portugal's parliament. Soon after, the trolley enters a relatively narrow street at the edge of the Bairro Alto.

Santa Catarina: A couple of stops into the Bairro Alto, this area is enjoyable for a stroll through characteristic streets downhill to the **Miradouro de Santa Catarina,** a view terrace with inviting cafés and bars.

Calhariz-Bica: Keep an eye on the streets to your right. You'll spot the top of the **Elevador da Bica funicular,** which drops steeply through a rough-and-tumble neighborhood to the riverfront.

City-Center Stops: From here, the downtown stops come fast and furious—**Chiado** (at Chiado's main square, Lisbon's café meeting-place); **Baixa** (on Rua da Conceição between Augusta and Prata); **Sé** (the cathedral); **Miradouro das Portas do Sol** (the Alfama viewpoint); **Campo de Santa Clara** (flea market on Tue and Sat); and the pleasant and untouristy **Graça** district (with two excellent viewpoints, one at Graça Church and another nearby at Nossa Senhora do Monte). The route finishes at **Praça Martim Moniz.**

Trolley #12E

For a colorful, 20-minute loop around the castle and the Alfama, catch trolley #12E on **Praça da Figueira** (departs every few minutes from the stop at corner of square closest to castle; runs about 8:00-20:45, shorter hours on Sat-Sun). The driver can tell you when to get out for the **Miradouro das Portas do Sol viewpoint** near the castle (about three-quarters of the way up the hill), or you can stay on the trolley and be dropped back where you started. Here's what you'll see on this loop ride:

Leaving Praça da Figueira, you enter **Praça Martim Moniz**—named for a knight who died heroically while using his body as a doorjamb to leave the castle gate open, allowing his Christian Portuguese comrades to get in and capture Lisbon from the Moors in 1147. These days, this gathering point is nicknamed "Dragon

Square" for the modern sculpture erected in the middle by the local Chinese community to celebrate the Year of the Dragon.

At the next stop, on the right, is the picturesque **Centro Comercial da Mouraria,** a marketplace filled with products and aromas from around the world. The big, maroon-colored building capping the hill on the left was a Jesuit monastery until 1769, when the dictatorial Marquês de Pombal booted the pesky order out of Portugal and turned the building into the Hospital São Jose. Today, this is an immigrant neighborhood with lots of cheap import shops.

Turning right onto Rua de Cavaleiros, you climb through the atmospheric **Mouraria neighborhood** on a street so narrow that a single trolley track is all that fits. Notice how the colorful mix of neighbors who fill the trolley all seem to know each other. If the trolley's path is blocked and can't pass, lots of horn-honking and shouts from passengers ensue until your journey resumes. Look up the skinny side streets. Marvel at the creative parking and classic laundry scenes. This was the area given to the Moors after they were driven out of the castle and Alfama. Natives know it as the home of the legendary fado singer Maria Severa as well as modern-day singer Mariza. The majority of residents these days are immigrants from Asia, making this Lisbon's most visible melting pot.

At the crest of the hill—at the square called **Largo Rodrigues de Freitas**—you can get out to explore, eat at a cheap restaurant (see "Eating in Lisbon," later), or follow Rua de Santa Marinha to the Campo de Santa Clara flea market (Tue and Sat).

When you see the river, you're at **Largo das Portas do Sol** (Gates of the Sun), where you'll also see the remains of one of the seven old Moorish gates of Lisbon. The driver usually announces *"castelo"* (cahzh-TAY-loo) at this point. Hop out here if you want to visit the Museum and School of Portuguese Decorative Arts (see page 32), enjoy the most scenic cup of coffee in town, explore the **Alfama,** or tour the **castle.**

The trolley continues downhill. First you'll pass (on the right) the stout building called **Aljube**—a prison built on a site dating from Roman times that, more recently, housed political opponents of Portugal's fascist dictator Salazar (now housing a museum about that regime; see page 57). Just downhill is the fortress-like **Lisbon Cathedral** (on the left—see page 56). Finally you roll into the Baixa (grid-planned Pombaline city—get off at **Praça do Comércio** to take my self-guided Baixa walk). After a few blocks, you're back where you started—Praça da Figueira.

Trolley #24E

Although it doesn't go past many of my recommended sights, a 20-minute ride on line #24E can show you a nice slice of workaday Lisbon (runs about 7:00-20:00, shorter hours on Sat-Sun). Catch the trolley at **Praça Luís de Camões** (just uphill from Chiado); ride past **Príncipe Real** and its beautiful park, prime shopping, and good restaurants; the enormous cistern at the end of the aqueduct; and the **Amoreiras** mall, ending in **Campolide**. Hop off and hop on again right away, or wander over to **Edward VII park** to stroll down the tree-lined Avenida da Liberdade to return to the city center.

Private Trolley Tours

Yellow Bus—the dominant local tour operator (see next)—operates two 1.5-hour hop-on, hop-off trolley tours that use the same tracks and stops as the public trolleys described above. Though pricier and less frequent than public trolleys, Yellow Bus trolley tours often have fewer crowds, come with recorded commentary, and allow you to hop on and off as often as you like for 24 hours. Both tours start at Praça do Comércio and run every 30 minutes (fewer off-season). There are two lines: Hills Tramcar Tour (€20, runs 9:30-19:00, 13 stops, red trolleys) and Belém Tramcar Tour (€15, runs 10:00-18:30, 9 stops, green trolleys).

Hop-On, Hop-Off Bus Tours

Various companies operate hop-on, hop-off bus tours around Lisbon. While uninspiring and not cheap—and Lisbon's sights are compact enough to easily see on your own—these tours can be handy and run daily year-round.

Yellow Bus (www.yellowbustours.com) and **Gray Line** (www.cityrama.pt) run multiple loops through town, targeting different sights; figure around €15 for 24 hours on one loop, or about €25 for 48-hour access to all loops. Each company also offers a dizzying array of combo- tickets (trolley tours, tuk-tuks, boat trips, Segway tours, museum discounts, and so on). Buses depart from Praça da Figueira (buy tickets from driver). When comparing your options, note that Yellow Bus tickets include some Lisbon city transit as well (public trolleys, buses, Elevador de Santa Justa, and funiculars, but not the Metro).

Tuk-Tuks

Goofy little tuk-tuks—Indian-style, three-wheel motorcycles—have invaded Lisbon. You'll see them parked in front of tourist landmarks all over town. They have no meter—negotiate with the driver for a tour or hire one for a point-to-point ride. Tuk-tuks are most practical as a way to tailor your own private tour (€45/hour, €30 if demand is slow and the driver owns his own rig). The key is finding a likeable driver with good language skills and a little charm. A ride comes with light guiding, can get you into little back

---

Ways to Get from the Baixa Up to the Bairro Alto and Chiado

- Ride the Elevador da Glória funicular (a few blocks north of Rossio on Avenida da Liberdade, opposite the Hard Rock Café), or hike alongside the tracks if the funicular isn't running.
- Walk up lots of stairs from Rossio (due west of the central column).
- Taxi or Uber to the Miradouro de São Pedro de Alcântara.
- Take the escalators at the Baixa-Chiado Metro stop. From outside the station on Rua do Crucifixo, you'll first ride down, then walk past the turnstiles for the Metro entrance, then ride back up, up, up.
- Catch trolley #28E from Rua da Conceição.
- Hike up Rua do Carmo from Rossio to Rua Garrett.
- Take the elevators inside the Armazéns mall (go through the low-profile doors at Rua do Crucifixo 89 or 113); ride to floor 5 and pop out at the bottom of Rua Garrett.
- Take the Elevador de Santa Justa, which goes right by the Convento do Carmo and Chiado (long lines at busy times—but if it's jammed, other options are nearby).

---

lanes, lets you hop on and off for quick visits and photo stops, and leaves you where you like.

BY BOAT

To get out on the Rio Tejo, take a sightseeing cruise or ride a public ferry. Either way, the main destination across the river is the port of Cacilhas.

Tourist Cruise: Yellow Boat—part of the big Yellow Bus tour company—offers a 1.5-hour loop that links Terreiro do Paço (near Praça do Comércio) to Belém. You can hop on and off, but there are just eight boats per day (€20/24 hours, discounts and combo-tickets with their bus tours and other offerings, May-Oct only, details at www.yellowbustours.com).

Public Ferry Ride to Cacilhas: For a quick, cheap trip across the river with great city and bridge views in the company of Lisbon commuters rather than tourists, hop the ferry to Cacilhas from the Cais do Sodré terminal. See page 88 for details.

ON FOOT

Two walking-tour companies—Lisbon Walker and Inside Lisbon—offer excellent, affordable tours led by young, top-notch guides with a passion for sharing insights about their hometown. Both have an easygoing style and small groups (generally 2-12 people); with either, you'll likely feel you've made a friend in your

Lisbon at a Glance

In Lisbon

▲▲▲**Alfama Stroll and the Castle** Tangled medieval streets topped by São Jorge Castle. See page 26.

▲▲▲**Baixa Stroll** The lower town—Lisbon's historic downtown—gridded with streets and dotted with major squares. See page 34.

▲▲▲**Bairro Alto and Chiado Stroll** The high town's views, churches, and Chiado fashion district. See page 46.

▲▲**Gulbenkian Museum** Lisbon's best museum, featuring an art collection spanning 5,000 years, from ancient Egypt to Impressionism to Art Nouveau. **Hours:** Wed-Mon 10:00-18:00, closed Tue. See page 60.

▲▲**Museum of Ancient Art** Portuguese paintings from the 15th- and 16th-century glory days. **Hours:** Tue-Sun 10:00-18:00, closed Mon. See page 65.

▲▲**Parque das Nações** Inviting waterfront park with a long promenade, modern mall, aquarium, and the Expo '98 fairgrounds. See page 86.

▲**Fado Museum** The story of Portuguese folk music. **Hours:** Tue-Sun 11:00-17:00, closed Mon. See page 34.

▲**São Roque Church and Museum** Fine 16th-century Jesuit church with false dome ceiling, chapel made of precious stones, and a less-interesting museum. **Hours:** Mon 14:00-18:00, Tue-Sun 9:00-19:00—until 18:00 in winter, Thu until 20:00. See page 48.

▲**Lisbon Cathedral** From the outside, an impressive Romanesque fortress of God; inside, not much. **Hours:** Tue-Sat 9:00-19:00, Sun-Mon until 17:00. See page 56.

▲**Aljube Museum of Resistance and Freedom** Exhibits documenting fascist António Salazar's rise to power, housed in a for-

guide. These tours can be time and money very well spent (both give my readers a discount).

Lisbon Walker

Standard tours include "Lisbon Revelation" (best 3-hour overview, with good coverage of Baixa and main squares, quick look at Bairro Alto, and trolley ride across town to Portas do Sol viewpoint); "Old Town" (2.5-hour walk through Alfama that examines the origins of

LISBON

mer prison building. **Hours:** Tue-Sun 10:00-18:00, closed Mon. See page 57.

▲**Mouraria District** Historic Moorish quarter turned buzzing international zone with inviting eateries. See page 59.

▲**National Tile Museum** Tons of artistic tiles, including a panorama of preearthquake Lisbon. **Hours:** Tue-Sun 10:00-18:00, closed Mon. See page 87.

In Belém
▲▲▲**Monastery of Jerónimos** King Manuel's giant 16th-century, white limestone church and monastery, with remarkable cloister and the explorer Vasco da Gama's tomb. **Hours:** Tue-Sun 10:00-18:30, Oct-April until 17:30, closed Mon. See page 73.

▲▲**National Coach Museum** Dozens of carriages, from simple to opulent, displaying the evolution of coaches from 1600 on. **Hours:** Tue-Sun 10:00-17:00, closed Mon. See page 70.

▲**Casa Pastéis de Belém** Sprawling café and bakery where you can enjoy Lisbon's famous custard tarts where they were first created. **Hours:** Daily 8:00-23:00. See page 72.

▲**Maritime Museum** Salty selection of exhibits on the ships and navigational tools of the Age of Discovery. **Hours:** Daily 10:00-18:00, Oct-April until 17:00. See page 79.

▲**Monument to the Discoveries** Giant riverside monument honoring the explorers who brought Portugal great power and riches centuries ago. **Hours:** Daily 10:00-19:00; Oct-April Tue-Sun until 18:00, closed Mon. See page 80.

▲**Belém Tower** Consummate Manueline building with a worthwhile view up 120 steps. **Hours:** Tue-Sun 10:00-18:30, Oct-April until 17:30, closed Mon. See page 83.

Lisbon); and "Downtown" (2-3 hours, covers 1755 earthquake and rebirth of Lisbon). Each tour includes a shot of *ginjinha* or a tasty *pastel de nata*—two edible icons of Lisbon (€20/person, RS%—€15 with this book; tours run daily year-round—check schedule online; meet at northwest corner of Praça do Comércio near Rua do Arsenal, in front of the TI—see map on page 35, +351 218 861 840, www.lisbonwalker.com).

Inside Lisbon

Tours include the "Best of Lisbon Walk" (good 3-hour highlights tour of the main squares, Chiado, and Alfama; €18/person, €13 with this book; daily year-round at 10:00) and food and wine tours (see "Food Tours," later). Most tours meet at the statue of Dom Pedro IV in the center of Rossio and last three to four hours (reserve a day ahead via website or phone, mobile +351 968 412 612, www.insidelisbon.com). They also offer daily private tours and day trips by minivan (€75/person, RS%—€5 discount with this book or online with code "RICKLISBON") to Sintra/Cascais (8 hours) and Obidos/Fátima (9 hours). You can organize a private city tour with them, or use their helpful website as a resource for seeing Lisbon on your own.

Lisbon Chill-Out Free Walking Tours

Many companies offer "free" tours, but most are led by expats who memorize a script and are cluttered with cross-selling and promotions. In the end, you'll be hit up hard for a tip. If you're looking for a free tour, I'd choose Chill-Out. Your Chill-Out guide is a local who will share cultural insights as you walk through the Bairro Alto, across the Baixa, and into the Alfama. It's refreshing to get a hometown perspective, and they are upfront about "it's not really free—you tip what you like at the end." Three-hour walks start in the Bairro Alto at the statue on Praça Luís de Camões (look for the guide wearing the yellow travel bag) daily at 10:00 and 15:00 (www.lisbonfreetour.blogspot.pt).

FOOD TOURS

Guided food tours are trendy these days. Several companies offer three- to four-hour multistop tours that introduce you to lots of local food culture while filling your stomach at the same time. This is a quickly evolving scene, so it pays to do a little homework on the latest offerings. But I've enjoyed tours by several good outfits, listed below. In each case, the groups are small, the teaching is good, and—when you figure in the cost of the meal—the tours are a solid value.

Inside Lisbon offers three food-related itineraries (RS%—€5 discount with this book): Their "Food and Wine Walk" makes five to six short, tasty, and memorable stand-up stops (€45/person, 3 hours, Mon-Sat at 16:30). The "Sunset, Fado, and Tapas" walk includes an evening stroll and samples of local food and music (€65/person, 4 hours, departs at 19:00, 5/week in summer, 2/week in winter). And their "Lisbon Experience Walk" is a tour through the Mouraria neighborhood with some food stops mixed in, ending with a ferry to Cacilhas for seafood (€45/person, 4 hours, Mon-Sat at 10:30; www.insidelisbon.com).

Taste of Lisboa food tours, designed by Filipa Valete, connects you with a Lisboan guide and offers a fast-moving feast with lots of visits and lots of information. Their primary tour is the "Lisbon Roots, Food & Culture Walk" with seven stops (€70/person, 4 hours, Mon-Sat at 15:00 and 15:45, 2 to 12 per group, English only, sign up at www.tasteoflisboa.com). They offer several other cultural food experiences, all explained on their website.

Eat Drink Walk does a €85 "Tapas Downtown" walk (3-4 hours, 5-6 stops in the Baixa), as well as a €95 "Chiado Gourmet" walk (4-5 hours, www.eatdrinkwalk.pt). Both tours run Mon-Sat at 11:30 and are expertly led by Filomena or Duarte, both locals and pioneers in the food tour world of Lisbon.

LOCAL GUIDES

Hiring a private local guide in Lisbon can be a wonderful luxury: Your guide will meet you at your hotel and tailor a tour to your interests. Especially with a small group, this can be a fine value. Guides charge roughly the same rates (€125/half-day, €200/day; car and driver options are available).

Cristina Quental works with a trio of good local guides (€150/half-day, €240/day, mobile +351 919 922 480, www.lisbon4smile.com, anacristinaquental@hotmail.com).

Claudia da Costa, who appears on my Lisbon TV show, is also excellent (mobile +351 965 560 216, claudiadacosta@hotmail.com).

Cristina Duarte knows Lisbon well, also appears on my TV show, and leads private tours in Lisbon when not on the road leading Portugal tours for my company (mobile +351 919 316 242, www.lisbonbeyond.pt, acrismduarte@gmail.com).

Teresa Ferreira works in Lisbon and the surrounding area (mobile +351 966 139 564, www.borninlisbon.com, maria-te@live.com.pt).

Your Friend in Lisbon is a group of four guides who book private three-hour walks for €120 (price for one or two, more for larger groups, daily at 11:00 or 15:00, mobile +351 919 292 151, www.yourfriendinlisbon.com, alex@yourfriendinlisbon.com, run by Alex Almeida). They also have a minivan and driver (€400 for all-day, for up to six).

Neighborhood Walks in Lisbon

The essential Lisbon is easily and enjoyably covered in three ▲▲▲ self-guided walking tours through three downtown neighborhoods: Alfama, Baixa, and Bairro Alto/Chiado. You can do them as individual walks, or lace them together into a single tour (allow a minimum of five hours for all three, but could be done as a more leisurely all-day experience—or, for maximum lingering, spread it over two days). You can do the walks in any order, but starting with the Alfama gets you to the castle before the crowds hit, kicking things off with a grand city view from Lisbon's fortified birthplace. And you'll finish in the liveliest quarter for evening fun—the Bairro Alto/Chiado.

🎧 My free Lisbon City Walk audio tour covers the same territory as the walks, from Praça do Comércio through the Baixa, and up through the highlights of the Bairro Alto (but not the Alfama or castle).

ALFAMA STROLL AND THE CASTLE

On this ▲▲▲ walk, you'll explore the Alfama, the colorful sailors' quarter that dates to the age of Visigoth occupation, from the sixth to eighth centuries AD. This was a bustling district during the Moorish period, and eventually became the home of Lisbon's fishermen and mariners (and of the poet Luís de Camões, who wrote, "Our lips meet easily, high across the narrow street"). The Alfama's tangled street plan, one of the few features of Lisbon to survive the 1755 earthquake, helps make the neighborhood a cobbled playground of Old World color. While much of the Alfama's grittiness has been cleaned up in recent years, it remains one of Europe's more photogenic neighborhoods.

When to Go: The best times to visit are during the busy midmorning market, or in the cooler late afternoon or early evening, when the streets teem with residents.

Getting There: This walk begins at the highest point in town, São Jorge Castle. Get to the castle gate by **taxi;** by **minibus #737** from Praça da Figueira; or by two free **elevator rides** up from the Baixa and then a short uphill walk. To find the elevators, head to Rua dos Fanqueiros and go through the easy-to-miss door at #178 (for location, see the map on page 35; you'll see faint, white lettering spelling out *elevador castelo* on the red rooftop—illuminated at night). Ride the elevator to the top floor and exit, angling left across the street and through the little square. Then head up Largo Chão do Loureiro, where you'll see the second elevator (*elevador castelo;* handy supermarket at bottom, view café and fine panoramic terrace at top). When exiting the second elevator, simply follow brown *Castelo de S. Jorge* signs up to the castle (right, then hooking left; about 8 minutes uphill).

❶ São Jorge Castle Gate and Fortified Castle Town

The formidable gate to the castle is part of a fortification that, these days, surrounds three things: the view terrace, the small town that stood within the walls, and the castle itself. The ticket office and

Alfama Stroll

❶ São Jorge Castle Gate & Fortified Castle Town
❷ Miradouro de São Jorge
❸ São Jorge Castle
❹ Castle Town
❺ Largo Santa Luzia
❻ Museum & School of Portuguese Decorative Arts
❼ Heart of the Alfama (Largo de São Miguel)
❽ Fado Museum

the turnstile are situated so that those without a ticket are kept away from the view terrace and castle proper (castle entry-€8.50, daily 9:00-21:00, Nov-Feb until 18:00).

If money is tight, the castle and view are skippable—the castle is just stark, rebuilt ruins from the Salazar era, and while the hill-capping park has a commanding view, there are other fine views coming up...just jump ahead to stop #4 on this walk.

LISBON

• If you decide to go in, follow the cobbles uphill past the first lanes of old Lisbon to the yellow ticket office, and then into the...

❷ Miradouro de São Jorge (Viewpoint)

Enjoy the grand view. The Rio Tejo is one of five main rivers in Portugal, four of which come from Spain. (Only the Mondego River, which passes through Coimbra, originates inside Portuguese territory, in the Serra de Estrela.) While Portugal and Spain generally have very good relations, a major sore point is the control of all this water. From here, you have a good view of the Golden Gate-like 25th of April Bridge, which leads south to the Cristo Rei statue. Past the bridge, on a clear day, you can barely see the Monument to the Discoveries and the Belém Tower (under and past the bridge on north side).

Look up at the statue marking the center of this terrace. **Afonso Henriques,** a warlord with a strong personal army, was the founder of Portugal. In 1147, he besieged this former Moorish castle until the hungry, thirsty residents gave in. Every Portuguese schoolkid knows the story of this man—a Reconquista hero and their country's first king.

Stroll inland along the **ramparts** for a more extensive view of Pombal's Lisbon, described in a circa 1963, tiled panorama-chart (which lacks the big 25th of April Bridge—it was built in 1969). From Praça do Comércio on the water, the grid streets of the Baixa lead up to the tree-lined Avenida da Liberdade and the big Edward VII Park, on the far right. Locate city landmarks, such as the Elevador de Santa Justa (the Eiffel-style elevator in front of the ruined Convento do Carmo) and the sloping white roof of Rossio station.

• Continue walking along the viewpoint, passing several old cannons. Just after going under the second arch (just before the café terrace), take a right into the mostly ruined courtyard of...

❸ São Jorge Castle (Castelo de São Jorge)

While the first settlements here go back to the 7th century BC, this castle dates to the 11th century when Moors built it to house their army and provide a safe haven for their elites in times of siege. After Afonso Henriques took the castle in 1147, Portugal's royalty lived here for several centuries. The sloping walls—typical of castles from this period—were designed to withstand 14th-century cannonballs. In the 16th century, the kings moved to their palace on Praça do Comércio, and the castle became a military garrison.

Despite suffering major damage in the 1755 earthquake, the castle later served another stint as a military garrison. In the 20th century, it became a national monument.

The strolling **peacocks** remind visitors that exotic birds like these came to Lisbon originally as trophies of the great 16th-century voyages and discoveries. (Today the jaded birds ignore the tourists and cry as if to remember some long-forgotten castle captives.)

Bear left to find the **inner castle**—the boxy, crenelated fort in the middle. There's little to see inside the empty shell, but it's fun to climb up the steep stone steps to scramble around the top of the ramparts and towers, with ever-changing views of Lisbon, the Alfama, and the castle itself. (Up top, you'll also find a thrillingly low-tech camera obscura, which is demonstrated twice hourly—times and languages posted.)

As you explore the castle's inner sanctum, imagine it lined with simple wooden huts. The imposing part of the castle is the exterior. The builders' strategy was to focus on making the castle appear so formidable that its very existence was enough to discourage any attack. If you know where to look, you can still see stones laid by ancient Romans, Visigoths, and Moors. The Portuguese made the most substantial contribution, with a wall reaching all the way to the river to withstand anticipated Spanish attacks.

When finished, head back out the inner castle gate, and continue straight ahead toward the castle's entrance. On your right, you'll pass the café, then the humble **museum.** This houses archaeological finds from the 7th century BC to the 18th century, with emphasis on the Moorish period in the 11th and 12th centuries. You'll also see 18th-century tiles from an age when Portugal was flush with money from the gold, diamonds, and sugarcane of its colony Brazil. While simple, the museum has nice displays and descriptions.

• *Leave the castle. Across the ramp from the castle entrance is a tidy little castle district, worth a wander for its peaceful lanes and a chance to enjoy the Manueline architecture.*

❹ Castle Town

Just outside the castle turnstile is the tiny neighborhood within the castle walls built to give Moorish elites refuge from sieges and, later, for Portuguese nobles to live close to their king. While it's

Pombal's Lisbon

In 1750, lazy King José I (r. 1750-1777) turned the government over to a minor noble, the Marquês de Pombal (1699-1782). Talented, ambitious, and handsome, Pombal was praised as a reformer, but reviled for his ruthless tactics. Having learned modern ways as the ambassador to Britain, he battled Church repression and promoted the democratic ideals of the Enlightenment, but enforced his policies with arrests, torture, and executions. He expelled the Jesuits to keep them from monopolizing the education system, put the bishop of Coimbra in prison, and broke off relations with the pope. When the earthquake of 1755 leveled the city, within a month Pombal had kicked off major rebuilding in much of today's historic downtown—featuring a grid plan for the world's first quake-proof buildings. In 1777, the king died, and the controversial Pombal was dismissed.

partly taken over by cute shops and cafés, if you wander up Rua de Santa Cruz do Castelo (to the left as you exit the castle) and stroll into its back lanes, you can enjoy a peaceful bit of Portugal's past. (Make a big clockwise loop back to where you entered—you can't get lost, as it's within the walls and there's only one way in or out.) Most of the houses date from the Middle Ages. Poking around, go on a cultural scavenger hunt. Look for: 1) clever, space-efficient, triangular contraptions for drying clothes (hint: see the glass bottle bottoms in the wall used to prop the sticks out when in use); 2) Benfica soccer team flag (that's the team favored by Lisbon's working class—a hint that the upper class no longer chooses to live here); 3) short doors that were tall enough for people back when these houses were built; and 4) noble family crests over doors—dating to when important families wanted to be close to the king.

When you're ready to leave, make your way back to where you started, and head down the ramp to return to the real world. On your way out, just before exiting the lower gate, notice the little statue in the niche on your right. This is the castle's namesake: **St. George** (São Jorge; pronounced "sow ZHOR-zh") hailed from Turkey and was known for fighting valiantly (he's often portrayed slaying a dragon). When the Christian noble Afonso Henriques called for help to eliminate the Moors from his newly founded country of Portugal, the Crusaders who helped him prayed to St. George...and won.

• *Exit the castle complex grounds through the large archway, follow the castle wall, then turn right down the second street, Travessa do Chão da Feira. Follow this striped lane downhill through **Largo do Contador Mor**. This small, car-clogged square has a Parisian ambience, some tour-*

isty outdoor restaurants serving grilled sardines, and the inviting little **Miss Can** *shop and eatery—where traditional Portuguese canned fish gets a modern twist (for ideas on lunching here, see page 124).*

Exit the square at the bottom, continue downhill 50 yards farther, pass the trolley tracks, and jog right around the little church to reach a superb Alfama viewpoint at...

❺ Largo Santa Luzia

From this square (with a stop for trolleys #12E and #28E), admire the panoramic view from the small terrace, **Miradouro de Santa Luzia**, where old-timers play cards and Romeos strum their guitars amid lots of tiles.

In the distance to the left, the **Vasco da Gama Bridge** (opened in 1998) connects Lisbon with new, modern bedroom communities south of the river.

At your feet sprawls the Alfama neighborhood. We'll head that way soon, to explore its twisty lanes. Where the Alfama hits the river, notice the recently built embankment. It reclaimed 100 yards of land from the river to make a modern port, used these days to accommodate Lisbon's growing cruise ship industry.

On the wall of the church behind you, notice two 18th-century **tile panels.** The one on the left shows the preearthquake Praça do Comércio, with the royal palace (on the left). It was completely destroyed in the 1755 quake. The other tile (10 steps away, to the right) depicts the reconquest of Lisbon from the Moors by Afonso Henriques. You can see the Portuguese hero, Martim Moniz, who let himself be crushed in the castle door to hold it open for his comrades. Notice the panicky Moors inside realizing that their castle is about to be breeched by invading Crusaders. It was a bad day for the Moors. (A stairway here leads up to a tiny view terrace with a café.)

For an even better city view, hike back around the church and walk out to the seaside end of the **Miradouro das Portas do Sol** catwalk. The huge, frilly building dominating the ridge on the far left is the Monastery of São Vicente, constructed around 1600 by the Spanish king Philip II, who left his mark here with this tribute to St. Vincent. A few steps away, next to a statue of St. Vincent, is a kiosk café where you can enjoy perhaps the most scenic cup of coffee in town.

• Across the street from the café, you'll find the...

❻ Museum and School of Portuguese Decorative Arts

The Museum and School of Portuguese Decorative Arts (Museu Escola de Artes Decorativas Portuguesas) offers a stroll through

a richly decorated, aristocratic household. The palace, filled with 15th- to 18th-century fine art, offers the best chance for visitors to experience what a noble home looked like during Lisbon's glory days (€4, Wed-Mon 10:00-17:00, closed Tue, Largo das Portas do Sol 2, +351 218 814 640, www.fress.pt). Inside, a coach on the ground level is "Berlin style," with a state-of-the-art suspension system, on leather straps. The grand stairway leads upstairs past 18th-century glazed tiles (Chinese-style blue-and-white was in vogue) into a world of colonial riches. Portuguese aristocrats had a special taste for "Indo-Portuguese" decorative arts: objects of exotic woods such as teak or rosewood, and inlaid with shell or ivory, made along the sea routes of the age.

From here, it's downhill all the way. From Largo das Portas do Sol (the plaza with the statue of local patron St. Vincent, near the kiosk café on the terrace), go

down the loooong **stairs** (Rua Norberto de Araújo, between the church and the catwalk). A few steps down on the left, under the big arch, notice the public WCs and the fun, vivid **cartoon mural** illustrating Lisbon's history (if you know the key dates, you can enjoy it even without understanding Portuguese).

The massive eighth-century **fortified wall** (on the right of the staircase) once marked the boundary of Moorish Lisbon. Consider that the great stones on your right were stacked here over a thousand years ago. At the bottom of the wall, continue downhill, then turn left at the railing...and go down more stairs.

• *Explore downhill from here. The main thoroughfare, a concrete stepped lane called* **Escadinhas de São Miguel,** *funnels you to the Alfama's main square.*

❼ Heart of the Alfama

This square, **Largo de São Miguel,** is the best place to observe a slice of Alfama life. When city leaders rebuilt the rest of Lisbon after the 1755 quake, this neighborhood was left out and consequently retains its tangled medieval streets.

If you've got the time, **explore the Alfama** from this central square. Its urban-jungle roads are squeezed into confusing alleys—

the labyrinthine street plan was designed to frustrate invaders. What was defensive then is atmospheric now. Bent houses comfort each other in their romantic shabbiness, and the air drips with laundry and the smell of clams. Get lost. Poke aimlessly, peek through windows, buy a fish. Locals hang plastic water bags from windows in the summer to keep away the flies. Favorite saints decorate doors to protect families. St. Peter, protector of fishermen, is big in the Alfama. Churches are generally closed, since they share a priest. As children have very little usable land for a good soccer game, this square doubles as the neighborhood playground.

The tiny balconies were limited to "one-and-a-half hands" in width. A strictly enforced health initiative was designed to keep

the town open and well-ventilated. If you see carpets hanging out to dry, it means a laundry is nearby. Because few homes have their own, every neighborhood has a public laundry and bathroom. Until recently, in the early morning hours, the streets were busy with residents in pajamas, heading for these public baths. Today, many younger people are choosing to live elsewhere, lured by modern conveniences unavailable here, and old flats with older residents are under the watchful eye of real estate developers. Many long-term

residents have been evicted due to landlords claiming "necessary reforms," only to sell the entire building for development as tourist housing. In just one generation, the Alfama is feeling the pressure of gentrification.

Traditionally the neighborhood here was tightly knit, with families routinely sitting down to communal dinners in the streets. Feuds, friendships, and gossip were all intense. Historically, when a woman's husband died, she would wear black for the rest of her life—a tradition that's just about gone.

The Alfama hosts Lisbon's most popular outdoor party dedicated to St. Anthony (whose feast day is June 13, but the party goes on all month). Imagine tables set up everywhere, bands playing, bright plastic flowers strung across the squares, and all the grilled sardines *(sardinhas grelhadas)* you can eat. The rustic paintings of festive characters (with hints of Moorish style) remind locals of past parties, and strings and wires overhead await future festival dates when the neighborhood will again be festooned with colorful streamers.

While there are plenty of traditional festivals here, the most action on the Alfama calendar is the insane, annual mountain-bike street race from the castle to the sea (which you can see hurtle by in two minutes on YouTube; search "Lisboa downtown race").

Continue exploring downhill from here. Just below the square you'll see A Baiuca, a recommended amateur fado restaurant. Then, a few steps farther downhill, you'll hit the cobbled pedestrian lane, **Rua São Pedro.** This darkest of the Alfama's streets, in nearly perpetual shade, was the logical choice for the neighborhood's fish market. Modern hygiene requirements (which forbid outdoor stalls) killed the market, but it's still a characteristic lane to explore.

• *Turn left and follow Rua São Pedro out of the Alfama to the square called Largo do Chafariz de Dentro and, across the street, the...*

❽ Fado Museum

This ▲ museum tells the story of fado in English—with a great chance to hear these wailing fisherwomen's blues. Three levels of wall murals show three generations of local fado stars, and the audioguide lets you listen to the Billie Holidays of Portugal (€5, includes audioguide, Tue-Sun 11:00-17:00, closed Mon, Largo do Chafariz de Dentro, +351 218 823 470, www.museudofado.pt).

• *This walk is over. To get back downtown (or to Praça do Comércio, where the next walk starts), walk a block to the main waterfront drag and cruise-ship harbor (facing the museum, go left around it) where busy Avenida Infante Dom Henrique leads back to Praça do Comércio (to the right). While it's a 15-minute walk or quick taxi ride to Praça do Comércio, just to the left is a bus stop; hop on any bus for two stops, and you're there in moments. (Also, bus #759 goes on to Praça dos Restauradores.)*

BAIXA STROLL

This ▲▲▲ walk covers the highlights of Lisbon's historic downtown, the Baixa, which fills a flat valley between two hills. The district slopes gently from the waterfront up to Rossio, Praça dos Restauradores, Avenida da Liberdade, and the newer town. The walk starts at Praça do Comércio and ends at Praça dos Restauradores.

• *Start your walk at the statue of King José I in the center of* **Praça do**

LISBON

Baixa Stroll

200 Meters
200 Yards

13 ELEVADOR DA GLÓRIA
OBELISK
AV. DA CONDES
R. PORTAS S. ANTÃO
COLISEU
S. ANT.
To Elevador do Lavra
CAL. NOVA...
Praça Martim Moniz
#12E & 28E
Martim Moniz
R. D'ARCO D. GRAÇA
RUA DE PALMA

Praça dos Restauradores
WALK ENDS
12 Restauradores
M
ABEP TICKET KIOSK
R. REGEDOR
9 Largo de São Domingos
NAT'L THEATER
8 QUERIOZ
7 SÃO DOMINGOS
RUA DA MOURARIA

ROSSIO TRAIN STATION
CALÇADA WORKER MEMORIAL
11
10
9
ROSSIO
Rossio (Praça Dom Pedro IV)
M Rossio
Rossio
Bus Tours B
Praça da Figueira
6
B
#12E &15E
M Rossio
#714
R. BORRATEM
SWEETS
To Alfama

Largo do Cadoval

R. C. DUQUE
R. D. DUQUE
R. DA CONDESA
R. DA OLIVIERA
RUA NOVA DA TRINDADE
R. DA TRINDADE
ARCH
R. T. DEZEMBRO
R. BESTEGA
CONVENTO DO CARMO
ELEVADOR STA. JUSTA
Largo do Carmo
TR. DO CARMO
RUA SANTA JUSTA
RUA DA PRATA
RUA DOS FANQUEIROS
RUA DA MADALENA
RUA DOS DOURADORES
B A I X A
RUA DA ASSUNÇÃO
5
ELEVATOR UP TO SÃO JORGE CASTLE
S. NICOLAU
To Alfama

CHIADO
To Bairro Alto
RUA GARRETT
R. DO CARMO
RUA AUREA
ARMAZÉNS DO CHIADO MALL
RUA DA VITORIA
R. SERPA PINTO
R. IVENS
R. S. FRAN.
Baixa-Chiado M
Baixa-Chiado
RUA DOS SAPATEIROS
R. DO CRUCIFIXO
R. DO OURO
RUA AUGUSTA
RUA DOS CORREEIROS
CONCEIÇÃO
#28E T
To Alfama

R. CARDOSO
RUA DO ALMADA
C. S. FRANCISCO
#28E T
"HIDDEN CHURCH"
RUA DE SÃO JULIÃO
4
MUDE
RUA DE CONCEIÇÃO
MARTINHO DA ARCADA CAFÉ
3

Praça do Município
RUA DO COMÉRCIO
ARCH OF TRIUMPH
LISBON WALKER
#15E T
Praça do Comércio B
Bus Tours
M

WALK BEGINS
WINE-TASTING CENTER
Tarreiro do Paço
1
2

AV. RIBEIRA DAS NAUS
To Cais do Sodré Station via Riverside Promenade
PILLARS
Rio Tejo

1 Praça do Comércio
2 Lisbon's Riverfront
3 Rua do Comércio
4 Rua de São Julião
5 Church of St. Nicholas
6 Praça da Figueira
7 Church of São Domingos
8 Largo de São Domingos
9 Ginjinha Bars (2)
10 Rossio Square
11 Rossio Station
12 Praça dos Restauradores
13 To Avenida da Liberdade & Pombal Statue

LISBON

Comércio. Find a spot of shade in José's shadow (or take cover under the arcades) and read a bit about the Baixa's history.

Background: After the disastrous 1755 earthquake, the Baixa district was rebuilt on a grid street plan. The uniform and utilitarian Pombaline architecture (named after the Marquês de Pombal, the chief minister who rebuilt the city—see sidebar, earlier) feels almost military. That's because it is. The Baixa was constructed by military engineers who had experience building garrison towns overseas. The new Lisbon featured the architecture of conquest—simple to assemble, economical, with all the pieces easy to ship. The 18th-century buildings you'd see in Mozambique and Brazil are interchangeable with those in Lisbon.

The buildings are all uniform, with the same number of floors and standard facades. They were designed to survive the next earthquake, with stone firewalls and wooden frameworks that had flexible crisscross beams. The priorities were to rebuild fast, cheap, and shake-proof.

If it had been left up to the people, who believed the earthquake was a punishment from God, they would have rebuilt their churches bigger and more impressive than ever. But Pombal was a practical military man with a budget, a timeline, and an awareness of his society's limits. Large churches didn't fit into the new, orderly grid. In those austere postearthquake days, Pombal got his way.

The Baixa has three squares—two preearthquake (Comércio and Rossio) and one added later (Figueira)—and three main streets: Prata (silver), Aurea (gold), and Augusta (relating the Portuguese king to a Roman emperor). The former maze of the Jewish quarter was eliminated, but the area has many streets named for the crafts and shops once found there.

The Baixa's pedestrian streets, inviting cafés, bustling shops, and elegant old storefronts give the district a certain charm. City-government subsidies make sure the old businesses stay around, but modern ones find a way to creep in. I find myself doing laps up and down Rua Augusta in a people-watching stupor. Its delightful ambience is perfect for strolling.

• *Now turn your attention to the square itself.*

❶ Praça do Comércio (Commerce Square)

At this riverfront square bordering the Baixa—along the gateway to Lisbon—ships used to dock and sell their goods. This was the site of Portugal's royal palace for 200 preearthquake years, but after the 1755 earthquake/tsunami/fire, the jittery king fled to more stable Belém, never to return. These days, government ministries ring Praça do Comércio. It's also the departure point for city bus and tram tours, and boats that cruise along the Rio Tejo. The area opposite the harbor was conceived as a residential neighborhood for the upper class, but they chose the suburbs. Today, the square has two names ("Palace Square" and "Commerce Square") and little real life. Locals consider it just a big place to pass through.

The statue is **José I,** the king who gave control of the government to his chief minister, the Marquês de Pombal. Built 20 years after the quake, it shows the king on his horse, with Pombal (on the medallion), looking at their port. The king on horseback strikes a heroic pose, bravely riding through the ground covered in snakes (a contrast to his actual behavior after the earthquake, refusing to sleep in a stone building ever again). The snakes actually hide support mechanisms for the heavy statue. Triumph and Fame toot the king's arrival, while a horse represents Portugal's European power and an elephant asserts the country's dominance in Asia. In its glory days, this city was where east met west. The statue proved such a success that it jump-started sculptor Joaquim Machado de Castro's career (see more at his museum in Coimbra).

The big arch marking the inland side of the square is Lisbon's **Arch of Triumph** (with Vasco da Gama on the left and Pombal on the right). Disregarding his usual austerity, Pombal restored some of the city's Parisian-style grandeur at this central approach into downtown.

Facing the Arch of Triumph, get oriented to a few landmarks on the square (moving from left to right):

At 9 o'clock is the cozy **Wines of Portugal Tasting Room,** a nonprofit wine-appreciation venue. About two dozen local wines are offered; English descriptions are above each tap, and a helpful attendant is happy to explain things. To taste, you buy a chip card (€3 minimum and €1 deposit for the card), take a glass, and serve yourself samples of Portuguese wines of every variety: white, red, green *(vinho verde),* and a few ports (each €1 and up; focused flights of five wines can be reserved for €8-15; daily 11:00-19:00).

At 10 o'clock is the **TI.**

At 2 o'clock, under the arcade just right of the arch, is **Martinho da Arcada,** a fine option for a coffee, pastry, or snack (Praça do Comércio 8, at the corner of Rua da Prata). It was founded in

1782—when the wealthy would come here to savor early ice cream made with mountain snow, lemon, and spices. While it has a fancy restaurant, I'd enjoy just a coffee and pastry in its café bar. This place was one of poet Fernando Pessoa's old haunts (they display a few Pessoa artifacts, lots of old photos, and a shrine-like table that was his favorite). In the early 20th century, painters, writers, and dreamers shared revolutionary ideas here over coffee.

At 3 o'clock is the much-promoted **"Lisbon Story Center,"** a childish exhibit with no artifacts—you pay €8 to stand for an hour looking at animated history on computer screens. Nearby is another branch of the **TI** (in case the first one is too crowded).

And at 5 o'clock is the **Terreiro do Paço Metro stop** (see the red *M* on a post). Finally, look up to see the tree-covered home to São Jorge Castle from the previous walk.

• *Before moving on, use the crosswalk at the bottom of the big square for a quick look at...*

❷ Lisbon's Riverfront

An inviting balustrade and a pair of Pombaline pillars—Lisbon's gateway to the sea, an arrival and departure point for everyone from Philip II of Spain to dictator António de Oliveira Salazar—mark a little pier (called the Cais das Colunas) that offers a fine, water-level view of the Tejo riverscape. To your left is the busy Terreiro do Paço ferry terminal—one of many that connect commuters to the far side of the river. To your right are the 25th of April Bridge and Cristo Rei statue. Down here at water level, you can really see that the Tejo is a tidal river—the Atlantic is just around the bend (past the bridge). At low tide, the humble little rocky beach reveals worlds of sea life in rocky pools. Any tide poolers out today?

• *Now, head back up through the square, cross the busy street, pass under the big arch, and walk down Rua Augusta into the Baixa district. (Skip the chance to pay to go to the top of the arch—it affords only a mediocre view from its empty rooftop.)*

The first cross-street you meet is...

❸ Rua do Comércio

Look right to see the old **cathedral** with its Romanesque fortress-like crenellations (described later, under "Sights in Lisbon"). Notice that many of the surrounding buildings are in the austere architectural style adopted immediately after the earthquake. Exterior decoration was adopted here in Lisbon only in the 19th century, after the Portuguese in colonial Brazil found that the tiles protected against humidity.

The characteristic black-and-white cobbled **sidewalk** *(calçada)* is uniquely Portuguese. These mosaic limestone and basalt cobbles were first cut and laid by 19th-century prison laborers, but maintaining them has since developed into a skilled craft. To this day patterns are chosen from acceptable designs made from large, wooden stencils. One benefit of these sidewalks is that they move and flow with the earth; even as tree roots spread or the ground shifts, the asphalt does not crack. But as the stones can be slippery and require skilled labor, the city government is talking about replacing them with modern pavement. Locals are crying out to keep the tradition.

Across the street, on the right, you'll pass the **MUDE,** Lisbon's museum of 20th-century design and fashion, occupying a former bank building (likely closed for renovation).

• *The next cross-street is...*

❹ Rua de São Julião

Churches blend into the postearthquake Baixa. There's one about 30 yards to the left down Rua de São Julião (hiding on right side

of street; look for the triangular pediment over door). Churches were rebuilt to be better incorporated into the no-nonsense grid plan of the Baixa. Look up for evidence of how downtown Lisbon's population is shrinking as more people move to the suburbs: The upper floors of many buildings are now mostly empty.

At the next block, **Rua da Conceição,** there's a stop for the handy trolley #28E. Ahead on the right (in the windows of the Millennium Bank) are Roman artifacts—a reminder that Lisbon's history goes way back.

• *Go two more blocks to the intersection with Rua da Vitoria. Turn right and walk two blocks to Rua da Prata, where you'll see the camouflaged...*

❺ Church of St. Nicholas (Igreja de São Nicolau)

Notice how a typical church facade faces the square, but on the

streetfront side, the entire exterior is covered with green tiles, as just another stretch of post-earthquake Baixa architecture. The church made extra income by leasing what is technically their property to the businesses on busy Rua da

Prata. Several of the fine, tiled buildings near this square have been refurbished. In fact, the one at the very top of the square hides a free elevator that takes you partway up to the castle atop the Alfama.

• *Head north down Rua da Prata toward the statue marking Praça da Figueira. At Rua de Santa Justa, look left for a good view of Elevador de Santa Justa before continuing straight to the square.*

❻ Praça da Figueira (Fig Tree Square)

This was the site of a huge hospital destroyed in the earthquake. With no money to replace the hospital, the space was left open until

the late 1880s, when it was filled with a big iron-framed market (similar to Barcelona's La Boqueria). That structure was torn down decades ago, leaving the square you see today.

The big building on the left, with its upper floors long neglected, has been purchased in part by Spanish tennis star Rafael Nadal for a total of €62 million. It's an example of the neighborhood being reinvigorated—though likely at the expense of long-time tenants.

The nearby **Confeitaria Nacional** shop (on the corner of the square, 20 yards to your left) is a venerable palace of sweets little changed since the 19th century. In the window is a display of "*conventuel* sweets"—special nun-made treats often consisting of sugar and egg yolks. (Historically, the nuns, who used the egg whites to starch their laundry, had an abundance of yolks.) Consider a light lunch in the recommended upstairs dining room.

The square is a transportation hub, with stops for minibus #737 to the castle; old trolley #12E to the Alfama viewpoint; modern trolley #15E and bus #714 heading out to Belém; and hop-on, hop-off tour buses.

Walk to the far-left corner of the square, past skateboarders oblivious to its historical statue—Portugal's King João I on a horse. Continue straight out of the square on **Rua Dom Antão de Almada**. This lane has several characteristic shops. Pop into the classic cod shop (on the left at #1C—you'll smell it). Cod *(bacalhau)* is part of Portugal's heritage as a nation of seafaring explorers: Salted cod could keep for a year on a ship. Just soak in water to rinse out the salt and enjoy. The adjacent ham counter serves *pata negra (presunto ibérico)* from acorn-fed pigs—the very best. Many say the *alheira* sausage, made with bread, game, and garlic instead of pork, was a favorite among Lisbon's Jews back when they needed to fake being

Christians (during the forced conversions of the Inquisition era). In reality, the sausage was a way to preserve other types of meat for long winter months.

• *At the end of the lane stands a big church facing another square.*

❼ Church of São Domingos

A center of the Inquisition in the 1600s, this is now one of Lisbon's most active churches (daily 7:30-19:00). The evocative interior—

rebuilt from the ruins left by the 1755 earthquake—would continue to play an important role in local history due to its location so near Rossio. Two famous royal weddings were held here in the 1800s. But the current state of the church—with black soot on the walls and charred stonework at the altar—is due to

a raging fire in 1959. Closed for decades, São Domingos finally reopened to the public in the 1990s, with all its scars still visible. Tabloid photos of fire damage can be seen at the exit. Our Lady of Fátima is Portugal's most popular saint, and her chapel (in the left rear of the church) always has the most candles. Her statue is accompanied by two of the three children to whom she miraculously appeared (the third was still alive when this chapel was made and so is not shown in heaven with the saint).

• *Step into the square just beyond the church.*

❽ Largo de São Domingos

This area was just outside of the old town walls—long a place where people gathered to keep watering holes busy and enjoy bohemian entertainment. Today the square is home to classic old bars (like the *ginjinha* bar described next) and a busy "eating lane," Rua das Portas de Santo Antão (kitty-corner from where you entered the square, to the right of the National Theater on the far side of the square).

    A stone monument on the square remembers the Jewish massacre of 1506. Many Jews expelled from Spain in 1492 took refuge in Portugal. But when a drought ravaged the country, Lisbonites killed several thousand of them on this square.

The city's 16th-century slave market also took place here, but the square is now a meeting point for the city's African community—immigrants from former Portuguese colonies such as Angola, Mozambique, and Portuguese Guinea. They hang out, trade news from home, and watch the tourists go by.

With that unfortunate heritage, the city today calls itself the "City of Tolerance." You'll see that phrase—in the language of all the communities that now live peacefully together here—on a wall behind the benches. Just beyond this square is a square called Praça Martim Moniz, the springboard for the tangled and characteristic Mouraria district, the immigrant neighborhood between here and the castle (described later, under "Sights in Lisbon").

• *Look toward the big adjoining square to find the colorful little tavern serving a traditional berry brandy.*

❾ Liquid Sightseeing (*Ginjinha* Bars)

Ginjinha (zheen-ZHEEN-yah) is a favorite Lisbon drink. While nuns baked sweets, the monks took care of quenching thirsts with this sweet liquor, made from the *ginja* berry (like a sour cherry), sugar, and brandy. It's now sold for €1.40 a shot in funky old shops throughout downtown. Buy it with or without berries (*com elas* or *sem elas*—that's "with them" or "without them") and *gelada* (if you want it poured from a chilled bottle). In Portu-

gal, when people are impressed by the taste of something, they say, "*Sabe que nem ginjas*"—literally "It tastes like *ginja*," but meaning "finger-lickin' good."

The oldest *ginjinha* joint in town is a hole-in-the-wall at Largo de São Domingos 8. If you hang around the bar long enough, you'll see them refill the bottle from an enormous vat. (Another *ginjinha* bar, Ginjinha Sem Rival, serves the prized *Eduardinho* liqueur, considered the most authentic; it's just across the square, at the start of the restaurant row—Rua das Portas de Santo Antão—at #7.)

• *A big square is around the corner (fronting the National Theater). This is...*

❿ Rossio Square

Lisbon's historic center, Rossio, is still the city's bustling cultural heart. Given its elongated shape, historians know it was a Roman racetrack 2,000 years ago; these days, cars circle the loop instead of chariots. It's home to the colonnaded National Theater, American fast-food chains, and street vendors who can shine your shoes, lam-

The Lisbon Earthquake of 1755

At 9:40 on Sunday, November 1—All Saints' Day—an underwater earthquake estimated to be close to 9.0 in magnitude occurred off the southern Portuguese coast. Massive tremors

rumbled through Lisbon, punctuated by three main jolts. The quake came midway through Mass, when devout locals filled the churches. Minutes later, thousands lay dead under the rubble.

Along the waterfront, shaken survivors scrambled aboard boats to sail to safety. They were met by a 20-foot wall of water, the first wave

of a tsunami that rushed up the Rio Tejo. The ravaging water capsized ships, swept people off the docks, crested over the seawall, and crashed 800 feet inland.

The tremors were felt throughout Europe—as far away as Finland. Imagine a disaster similar to 2004's Indian Ocean earthquake and tsunami, devastating Portugal's capital city.

Fires turned the city into an inferno. The flames blazed for five days, ravaging the downtown from the Bairro Alto across Rossio to the castle atop the Alfama.

Of Lisbon's 270,000 citizens, over 10,000 may have perished, and two-thirds of the city was leveled. The city's biggest buildings—its churches, designed to connect earth with heaven—had simply collapsed, crushing the faithful. Understandably, the quake shook conservative Portugal's moral and spiritual underpinnings. Had God punished Lisbon for the Inquisition killings carried out on nearby Praça do Comércio? To the people of the time, it must have felt like the Apocalypse.

King José I was so affected by the earthquake that he moved his entire court to an elaborate complex of tents in the foothills of Belém and resisted living indoors for the rest of his life. He left his energetic (and eventually dictatorial) second-in-command—his chief minister Marquês de Pombal—the task of rebuilding. For more on Pombal, see "Pombal's Lisbon," earlier.

inate your documents, and sell you cheap watches, autumn chestnuts, and lottery tickets. The column in the square's center honors Pedro IV—king of Portugal and emperor of Brazil. (Many maps refer to the square as Praça Dom Pedro IV, but residents always just call it Rossio, for the train station at one corner.)

The square once held a palace that functioned as the headquarters of the Inquisition. Damaged by the 1755 earthquake, it was demolished, and in an attempt to erase its memory, the National Theater was built in its place.

From here you can see the Elevador de Santa Justa and the ruined convent breaking the city skyline. Notice the fine stone patterns in the pavement—evoking waves encountered by the great explorers. (If you're prone to seasickness, don't look down as you cross the square.)

• *Crossing the square in front of the National Theater, you see...*

⓫ Rossio Station

The circa-1900 facade of Rossio station is Neo-Manueline. You can read the words *"Estação Central"* (central station) carved on its strik-

ing horseshoe arches. Find the empty niche where a statue of King Sebastian once stood in the center of two arches. Unfortunately, the statue fell and broke into many pieces in 2016 when a tourist climbed the facade to take a selfie (I'm not kidding). It has since been repaired but has yet to return...much like his legend. This romantic, dashing, and young soldier-king was lost in 1580 in an ill-fated crusade to Africa. As Sebastian left no direct heir, the crown ended up with Philip II of Spain, who became Philip I of Portugal. The Spanish king promised to give back the throne if Sebastian ever turned up—and ever since, the Portuguese have dreamed that Sebastian will return, restoring their national greatness. Even today, in a crisis, the Portuguese like to think that their Sebastian will save the day—he's the symbol of being ridiculously hopeful.

• *Just uphill from Rossio station is Praça dos Restauradores, at the bottom of Lisbon's long and grand Avenida da Liberdade. Between Rossio station and the square is Lisbon's oldest hotel, the **Avenida Palace.** Built as a terminus hotel at the same time as Rossio station, it has a fun interior, with an elegant yet inviting oasis of a bar/lounge—popular with WWII spies in the 20th century, and tourists needing a little break in the 21st century (nice after this walk).*

⓬ Praça dos Restauradores

This monumental square connects Rossio with Avenida da Liberdade. The obelisk at its centerpiece celebrates the restoration of

Lisbon's Kiosks

The kiosk—that's *quiosque* in Portuguese—is a standard feature of squares and viewpoints all over town. These little pavilions got their start in the 19th century selling snacks and drinks. But they fell out of favor, with some being converted to newsstands or lottery sales points. Now they're back, with outdoor cafés turning parks and squares into neighborhood hangouts and meeting points. Older kiosks have been restored, and new ones are being built all the time and can be quite trendy.

Portuguese independence from Spain in 1640 (without any help from the still-missing Sebastian mentioned earlier).

Looking uphill at the lower left corner of the square, find a statue remembering the generations of laborers who made the city's characteristic black-and-white *calçada* sidewalks. Lisboners love the patterns decorating their pavements throughout the town. Here, these bronze workers have made the symbol of the city: a ship, carrying the remains of St. Vincent, guarded by two ravens.

Overlooking the square is the 1930s Art Deco facade of the Eden Theater. About 100 yards farther up the boulevard (past a Metro station and TI, on the left) is the Elevador da Glória funicular that climbs to the Bairro Alto.

• *While this walk ends here, you can stroll up Avenida da Liberdade for a good look at another facet of this fine city. The next walk (Bairro Alto and Chiado Stroll) starts at the funicular just up the street on your left.*

⓭ Avenida da Liberdade

This tree-lined grand boulevard, running north from Rossio, connects the old town (where most of the sightseeing action is) with the newer upper town. Before the great earthquake, this was the city's royal promenade. After 1755, it was the grand boulevard of Pombal's new Lisbon—originally limited to the aristocracy. The present street, built in the 1880s and inspired by Paris' Champs-Elysées, is lined with hotels, high-fashion shopping, expensive office buildings...and eight lanes of traffic. The grand "rotunda"—as the roundabout formally known as Marquês de Pombal is called—tops off Avenida da Liberdade with a commanding **statue of Pombal**. Allegorical symbols of his impressive accomplishments decorate the statue. (An absent king and an iron-willed minister left in charge can do a lot in 27 years.) Beyond that lies the fine Edward VII Park. From the Rotunda (M: Marquês de Pombal), it's an enjoyable 20-minute downhill walk along the mile-long avenue back to the Baixa.

Whether strolling uphill or down, one of the joys of modern Lisbon is to simply walk this grand boulevard, dotted with monuments, statues, and food kiosks with inviting seating—perfect for enjoying a drink or snack.

BAIRRO ALTO AND CHIADO STROLL

The Old World-feeling Bairro Alto (High Town) and trendy Chiado perch just above the busy Baixa. This walk (rated ▲▲▲) connects dramatic viewpoints, leafy parks with inviting kiosk cafés, skinny streets lined with fado clubs, a dramatic church, an earthquake-toppled convent, Chiado's trendy dining and shopping scene, and a classic coffee house.

Getting There: Rise above the Baixa on the funicular called Elevador da Glória, located near the obelisk at Praça dos Restauradores (opposite the Hard Rock Café, €3.70 for two trips if you pay driver, €1.30 if zapping with Viva Viagem card, every 10 minutes); you can also hike up alongside the tracks.

• *Leaving the funicular on top, turn right (go 100 yards, up into a park) to enjoy the city view from the...*

❶ Miradouro de São Pedro de Alcântara (Viewpoint)

A tile map guides you through the view, which stretches from the twin towers of the cathedral (on far right, near the river), to the

ramparts of the castle birthplace of Lisbon (capping the hill, on right), to another quaint, tree-topped viewpoint in Graça (directly across, end of trolley #28E), to the skyscraper towers of the new city in the distance (far left). Whenever you see a big old building in Lisbon, it's often a former convent or monastery. With the dissolution of monastic religious orders in 1834, these buildings were nationalized and are now occupied by hospitals, museums, schools, or the military.

Bairro Alto & Chiado Stroll

❶ Miradouro de São Pedro de Alcântara
❷ Bairro Alto Detour
❸ São Roque Church
❹ Cervejaria da Trindade
❺ Largo do Carmo
❻ Convento do Carmo
❼ Elevador de Santa Justa
❽ Café A Brasileira
❾ Rua Garrett

In the park, a bust honors a 19th-century local journalist (founder of Lisbon's first daily newspaper) and a barefooted delivery boy. This district is famous for its writers, poets, publishers, and bohemians.

• *Directly across the street from where you got off the Elevador da Glória is* **Solar do Vinho do Porto**, *run by the Port Wine Institute—a good place to sample the famous fortified wine from northern Portugal (it's been closed for renovation but should reopen by the time you visit). If it's open, step inside—or consider returning later for a do-it-yourself tasting (for a description, see page 101).*

Next, walk directly across from the top of the funicular for a short detour into the old grid-plan streets of the Bairro Alto.

❷ Bairro Alto Detour

The Bairro Alto is one of the most characteristic and appealing districts in Lisbon. Designed in the 16th century with a very modern (at the time) grid-plan layout, the district housed ship workers back when Portugal was a world power and its ships planted the Portuguese flag all around the globe. Today, the Bairro Alto is quiet in the morning, but buzzes with a thriving restaurant scene in the evening and a rowdy bar scene later—much to the chagrin of elder residents.

While it's fun to wander, follow this route for a good sampling: Go two blocks gently uphill on Travessa da Boa Hora, turn left on Rua da Atalaia, continue three blocks, and then head left down Travessa da Queimada until you cross the big street (leaving the Bairro Alto) and reach the small square, Largo Trindade Coelho.

• *On Largo Trindade Coelho is the...*

❸ São Roque Church (Igreja São Roque)

Step inside and sit in a pew in the middle to take it all in (free; Mon 14:00-18:00, Tue-Sun 9:00-19:00—until 18:00 in winter, Thu until 20:00). Built in the 16th century, the ▲ church of St. Roque—dedicated to the saint who protects the faithful from disease and plagues—is one of Portugal's first Jesuit churches. The painted-wood, false-domed ceiling is perfectly flat. The acoustics here are top-notch, important in a Jesuit church, where

the emphasis is on the sermon. The numbered panels on the floor were tombs, nameless because they were for lots of people. They're empty now—the practice was stopped in the 19th century when parishioners didn't want plague victims rotting under their feet.

Survey the rich side chapels. The highlight is the **Chapel of St. John the Baptist** (left side of church, gold and blue lapis lazuli columns). It looks like it came right out of the Vatican...because it did. Made in Rome from precious materials, the chapel was the site of one papal Mass before it was disassembled and shipped to Lisbon. Per square inch, it was the most-costly chapel ever constructed in Portugal. Notice the mosaic floor (with the spherical symbol of Portugal) and, on the walls, three intricate, beautiful mosaics—a Vatican specialty, designed to take the place of real paintings, which were vulnerable to damage from candle smoke and incense. Notice also the delicate "sliced marble" symmetry and imagine the labor involved in so artfully cutting that stone five centuries ago.

The chapel to the left of St. John the Baptist features a riot of babies. Individual chapels—each for a different noble family—seem to be in competition. Keep in mind that the tiles are considered as extravagant as the gold leaf and silver. To the left of the main altar, a glass case is filled with relics trying to grab your attention.

Between the Chapel of St. John the Baptist and the relics, find the **sacristy** where, along with huge chests of drawers for vestments, you can see a series of 17th-century paintings illustrating scenes from the life of St. Francis Xavier—one of the founders of the Jesuit order along with St. Ignatius of Loyola and Peter Faber (irregular hours, only open when staffed).

On your way out, you might pop a coin into a rack of fake candles and power a prayer.

The **São Roque Museum** (Museu de Arte Sacra) to the left as you leave the church, is more interesting than your typical small church museum (€2.50, same hours as the church). It's filled with perhaps the best-presented collection of 16th- and 17th-century church art in town, and it's well-described in English. The church and this art, rare survivors of the 1755 earthquake, illustrate the religious passion that accompanied Portugal's Age of Discovery, with themes including the mission of the Jesuits and their response to the Reformation; devotion to relics; and devotion to the Virgin.

• *Back outside in the church square (WC underground), visit the statue of a friendly lottery-ticket salesman. Two lottery kiosks are nearby. Locals who buy into the Totoloto (which, like lotteries everywhere, is a form of taxation on gamblers that helps fund*

social outreach programs) rub the statue's well-polished ticket for good luck.

Continue (kitty-corner left across the square) downhill along Rua Nova da Trindade, following the tram tracks. At #20 (on the left), pop into...

❹ Cervejaria da Trindade

The famous "oldest beer hall in Lisbon" is worth a visit for a look at its 19th-century tiles. The beautifully tiled main room, once a dining hall for monks, still holds the pulpit from which the Bible was read as the monks ate. After monastic orders were abolished in 1834, the monastery became a brewery—you'll notice that while the oldest tiles have Christian themes, the later ones (from around 1860) are all about the beer. Among the Portuguese beers on tap are Sagres, the standard lager; Sagres Preta, a good dark beer (like a porter); and Bohemia, which is sweet, with more alcohol. At the bar in front you can get a snack and beer, while more expensive dining is in the back (see page 126).

• *Continue down the hill. You'll pass the recommended **Bairro do Avillez**—one of more than a dozen Lisbon eateries owned by celebrity chef José Avillez, who is helping to bring traditional recipes (like the ones at the cervejaria we just left) into the 21st century.*

Continue until the next intersection, where signs point left to the ruined Convento do Carmo. Follow the inside trolley tracks downhill and to the left. Just before you reach the square, notice (on the left) the well-stocked music shop—selling (among other instruments) the unique Portuguese guitars used to perform fado music.

You'll wind up in the leafy, inviting square called...

❺ Largo do Carmo

On this square decorated with an old fountain, lots of pigeons, and jacaranda trees from South America (with purple blossoms in June), police officers guard the headquarters of the National Guard. Famous among residents, this was the last refuge of the dictatorial Salazar regime. The Portuguese people won their freedom in 1974, in a peaceful uprising called the Carnation Revolution. The name came when revolutionaries placed flowers in the guns of the soldiers, making it clear it was time for democracy here. For more history, see the sidebar.

• *On Largo do Carmo, check out the ruins of...*

The Carnation Revolution

António de Oliveira Salazar, who ruled Portugal from 1926 to 1968, was modern Europe's longest-ruling dictator (he died in 1970). Salazar's authoritarian regime, the Estado Novo, continued in power under Prime Minister Marcelo Caetano until 1974.

By the 1970s, fighting in Portugal's far-flung colonies over the previous decade had demoralized much of Salazar's military, and at home, there was a growing appetite for a modern democracy. On April 25, 1974, several prominent members of the military decided it was time to oust the government. Their withdrawal of government support spelled the end of the Salazar era. Five people died that April day, in a well-planned, relatively bloodless coup. Citizens spilled into the streets to cheer and put flowers in soldiers' rifle barrels, giving the event its name: the Carnation Revolution. Suddenly, people were free to speak aloud what they formerly could only whisper in private.

In the revolution's aftermath, the country struggled to get the hang of democratic practices. Its economy suffered as overseas colonies fell to nationalist uprisings, with some 800,000 immigrants taking advantage of democratic Portugal's attempt to make amends for colonial wars: immediate citizenship. For colonial overlords, life went from "shrimp day and night" to a sudden collapse of the empire; for their own safety, they fled back to Portugal. A good number of these "returnees" didn't fit into their newly democratic old country. Feeling like people without a homeland, many ultimately left Portugal (joining Salazar's henchmen, who took refuge in Brazil). Even those who stayed were generally pro-dictator and angry about the revolution, contributing to a polarization of modern Portuguese society that exists to this day.

In 1976, the Portuguese adopted a constitution that separated church and state. These changes helped to break down an almost medieval class system and established parliamentary law. Mario Soares, a former enemy of the Salazar regime, became the new prime minister, ruling as a stabilizing presence through much of the next two decades. Today, Portugal is enthusiastically democratic.

⑥ Convento do Carmo

After the convent was destroyed by the 1755 earthquake, the Marquês de Pombal directed that the delicate Gothic arches of its church be left standing—supporting nothing but open sky—as a permanent reminder of that disastrous event. If you pay to enter, you'll see a fine memorial park in what was the nave, and (filling the former apse at the far end) a simple museum with Bronze Age and Roman artifacts, medieval royal sarcophagi, and a couple of Peruvian mummies—all explained in English (€4—cheapskates can do a deep knee-bend at the ticket desk, sneak a peek, and then crawl away; Mon-Sat 10:00-19:00, Oct-May until 18:00, closed Sun year-round).

• *Facing the convent, take the little lane that cuts around its right side. Head up the stairs next to the Bella Lisa Elevador restaurant to reach the gray, iron...*

❼ Elevador de Santa Justa

In 1902, an architect who had studied under Gustav Eiffel completed this 150-foot-tall iron elevator, connecting the lower and upper parts of town. The elevator's Neo-Gothic motifs are an attempt to match the ruined church near its top. It's free to peer through the railings from the entry-level ramp, but I'd spring for a ticket to climb the spiral stairs up to the top-floor lookout—with unobstructed views over the city (for details, see the sight listing on page 57).

Stroll around this celebration of the Industrial Age, enjoy the view, then retrace your steps to the square in front of the convent. (The nearby Leitaria Académica, a venerable little working-class eatery with tables spilling onto the delightful square, can be handy for a pricey snack or drink.)

• *Continue straight up through Largo do Carmo, walking a block slightly uphill on Travessa do Carmo. At the next square, take a left on Rua Serpa Pinto, walking downhill to Rua Garrett, where—in the little pedestrian zone 50 yards uphill on the right—you'll find a famous old café across from the Baixa-Chiado Metro stop.*

❽ Café A Brasileira

Slinky with Art Nouveau decor, this café is a 100-year-old institution for coffeehouse junkies. A Brasileira was originally a shop selling Brazilian products, a reminder that this has long been the city's shopping zone. Drop in for a *bica* (Lisbon slang for espresso) or a *pingado* (with a dollop of steamed milk; either costs €0.70 at the bar). A *pastel de nata* custard tart costs just €1.30—but the best place in downtown for one is just a short walk away (see "Exploring More of the Bairro Alto," later). WCs are down the stairs near the entrance.

The statue out front is of the poet

Fernando Pessoa, making him a perpetual regular at this café. He was the literary and creative soul of Lisbon in the 1920s and 1930s, when the country's avant-garde poets, writers, and painters would hang out here.

At the neighboring **Baixa-Chiado Metro stop,** a slick series of escalators whisks people effortlessly between Chiado Square and the Baixa. It's a free and fun way to survey a long, long line of Portuguese—but for now, we'll stay in the Chiado neighborhood. (If you'll be coming for fado in the evening—recommended places are nearby—consider getting here by zipping up the escalator.)

• *The Chiado district is popular for its shopping and theaters. Browse downhill on...*

❾ Rua Garrett

As you stroll, notice the mosaic sidewalks, ironwork balconies, and fine shops. The streetlamps you see are decorated with the symbol

of Lisbon: a ship, carrying the remains of St. Vincent, guarded by two ravens.

As you walk, peek into classy stores, such as the fabric lover's paradise **Paris em Lisboa**—imagine how this would have been the ultimate in *ooh là là* fashion in the 19th century (at #77, on the right). The next cross street, Rua Serpa Pinto, leads (in one block) to the **São Carlos Theater**—Lisbon's opera house. Celebrity chef José Avillez, whose eatery we passed earlier, and his culinary rivals have revitalized this sleepy quarter with several restaurants. (Avillez's Belcanto has often appeared high on the list of the "50 Best Restaurants in the World.") Between here and the theater is the recommended **Burel Mountain Originals,** selling traditional and modern Portuguese wool and flannel products (see "Shopping in Lisbon," later).

Continuing along Rua Garrett, at the next corner (after the church, at #73) is the venerable **Bertrand** bookstore—according to Guinness, the oldest bookstore in continuous operation (since 1732) with English books and a good guidebook selection. **A Vida Portuguesa**—my favorite shop for Portuguese gifts (quality textiles, soaps, home decor, sardines, wine, and so on) is at the end of the street behind the bookstore (Rua Anchieta 11).

Along the main drag, you'll start to see more and more international chains before Rua Garrett ends abruptly at the entrance of the big **Armazéns do Chiado mall.** This grand, six-floor shopping center connects Lisbon's lower and upper towns with a world of ways to spend money (including a handy food court on the sixth

Portugal's Greatest Poets

The Portuguese are justifiably proud of their two most famous poets, whose names, works, and memorials you may encounter in your travels.

Portugal's most important poet, **Luís de Camões** (1524-1580), was a Renaissance-age equivalent of ancient Greece's Homer. Camões' masterpiece, *The Lusiads (Os Lusíadas)*, tells the story of an explorer far from home. But instead of Odysseus, this epic poem describes the journey of Vasco da Gama, the man who found the route from Europe to India. Camões—who had sailed to Morocco to fight the Moors (where he lost an eye), to Goa (where he was imprisoned for debt), and to China (where he was shipwrecked)—was uniquely qualified to write about Portugal's pursuit of empire on the high seas. For more on Camões, see page 75.

Fernando Pessoa (1888-1935) used multiple personas in his poetry. He'd take on the voice of a simple countryman and express his love of nature in free verse. Or he'd write as an erudite scholar, sharing philosophical thoughts in a more formal style. By varying his voice, he was able to more easily explore different viewpoints and truths. While Pessoa loved the classics—reading Milton, Byron, Shelley, and Poe—he was a true 20th-century bohemian at heart. Café A Brasileira, where he'd often meet with friends, has a statue of Pessoa outside. Today, fado musicians still remember Pessoa, paying homage to him by putting his poetry into the Portuguese version of the blues.

floor). For Italian-style gelato, locals like **Santini em Casa,** a few steps downhill to the left as you face the mall (at #9).

• *Our walk is over. Whether you leave the Bairro Alto or stay to explore, directions are below.*

Leaving the **Bairro Alto:** To get from the mall to the Baixa—the lower town—take the elevator (press 1) down to the ground level. To get

from the mall to the Metro, exit through the lowest floor of the mall, turn
right, and walk 50 yards to the Baixa-Chiado Metro stop.

Or, if you have time and interest, consider...

Exploring More of the Bairro Alto

A short walk from the mall gives you a more complete look at this
high-altitude neighborhood and a scenic viewpoint. Backtrack
(heading west) up Rua Garrett to the
square **Praça Luís de Camões,** where
the great writer stands on a pillar, lean-
ing on a sword—more warrior than
poet.

Left of Camões, head uphill along
Rua do Loreto. Just where the square
and street meet, on the right at #2, notice the hubbub at the recommended
Manteigaria, which serves downtown's best *pastel de nata* custard tart.
Even if it's crowded, you'll typically
get served quickly (cashiers come along
the line to take your order). Pastry in
hand, shimmy down the narrow hall inside, where you can stand
at the counter and watch the pastry chefs in action—perpetually
cutting cross-sections of delicate dough, pressing it into little tins,
filling the pastries with gooey custard, and popping big trays into
the oven (at 750 degrees Fahrenheit, to get just the right amount
of caramelizing on top). Be sure to sprinkle your piping-hot pastry
with powdered sugar and cinnamon.

Continue three more blocks on Rua do Loreto, passing the
picturesque **Elevador da Bica funicular.** Then, one block farther,
turn left on Rua Marechal
Saldanha to reach the **Miradouro de Santa Cata-
rina,** a terrace—flanked
by bars—that overlooks
the city's harbor and river.
This is a popular hangout
for the dreadlocked gra-
nola crowd on a balmy
evening. You'll see a mon-

ument to the Cape of Good Hope (a.k.a. the Cape of Torment) that
personifies the cape as a monster. This mythic treatment was popu-
larized by poet Camões' *The Lusiads,* which celebrated and nearly
deified the great explorers of Portugal's Age of Discovery (such as
Vasco da Gama, portrayed as Ulysses), who had to overcome such
demons in their conquest of the sea.

Sights in Lisbon

CENTRAL LISBON

To get a full picture of the best of central Lisbon, take the three neighborhood walks (covering the Bairro Alto, Alfama, and Baixa; see earlier). Several central Lisbon sights are described in detail in those self-guided walks: São Jorge Castle, the Museum and School of Portuguese Decorative Arts, and the Fado Museum (in "Alfama Stroll and the Castle"), and the São Roque Church and Museum (in "Bairro Alto and Chiado Stroll").

▲Lisbon Cathedral (Sé de Lisboa)

The cathedral, just a few blocks east of Praça do Comércio, is not much on the inside, but its fortress-like exterior has been through as many refits as there are styles of architecture. The final remodel during the Salazar years turned the facade into a textbook example of the stark and powerful Romanesque "fortress of God." Twin, castle-like, crenellated towers solidly frame an impressive rose window.

Cost and Hours: Free, Tue-Sat 9:00-19:00, Sun-Mon until 17:00. You can pay extra to visit the cloister (€2.50) and treasury (€2.50), but I'd skip them unless you dig archaeology or fancy gold monstrances. It's on Largo da Sé, several blocks east of the Baixa—take Rua da Conceição east, which turns into Rua de Santo António da Sé. Trolleys #12E and #28E stop right out front, where the square is clogged with tuk-tuks offering tours around town.

Visiting the Church: Started in 1150, this was the first place of worship that Christians built after they retook Lisbon from the Moors. Located on the former site of a mosque, it made a powerful statement: The Reconquista was here to stay. The church is also the site of the 1195 baptism of St. Anthony—a favorite saint of Portugal (locals appeal to him for help in finding a parking spot, true love, and lost objects). Naturally for Portugal, tile panels around the baptismal font (in the back-left corner) portray St. Anthony preaching to the fish. Also, some of St. Vincent is buried here—legend has it that in the 12th century, his remains were brought to Lisbon on a ship guarded by two sacred black ravens, the symbol of the city. Take a stroll through the vast, dark interior—with rounded arches and a dim, windowless nave, it's quintessentially Romanesque. Near the altar, the darkness gives way to a slightly lighter Baroque zone. Here you can pay to enter the ambulatory and peaceful **cloister** (an archaeological work-in-progress—they're currently uncovering Roman ruins). The humble **treasury,** back near the entrance, is worth its fee only if you want to climb some stairs and see a silver box containing what's left of St. Vincent.

▲Aljube Museum of Resistance and Freedom (Museu do Aljube)

This museum is the best place to learn about Portugal's troubled mid-20th century. It fills a stern building called the Aljube (from a Moorish word meaning "waterless well"), immediately behind the cathedral. Once a Muslim prison, then a jail during the Inquisition (and on a site that dates back to Roman times), the Aljube later became the main political prison of Portugal's fascist regime under António Salazar. Today, it houses a modern, well-presented, three-floor exhibit detailing Salazar's rise to power, the creation of the Estado Novo, crimes against the Portuguese people, and the eventual end of the regime with the 1974 Carnation Revolution. Exhibits tell the story (in English) with photos and subtitled video clips, as well as some original documents and other artifacts. While often overshadowed by Franco in Spain and the communist regimes of eastern Europe, Salazar was hardly a Boy Scout—and this much-needed museum documents his abuses, filling a gap for those with an appetite for recent history.

Cost and Hours: €3, free Sun before 14:00, open Tue-Sun 10:00-18:00, closed Mon, Rua de Augusto Rosa 42, +351 218 172 400, www.museudoaljube.pt. The entrance is tucked under a tall staircase, on a little square with a stop for trolleys #12E and #28E, between the cathedral and the Alfama.

Elevador de Santa Justa (Santa Justa Elevator)

This 150-foot-tall iron tower, built in 1902, connects the flat Baixa district with the Bairro Alto/Chiado districts up above. One of the

city's main landmarks, it offers a sweat-free connection to the upper town, as well as a fine city view up top. You can climb to the rooftop lookout alone (and skip the elevator ride) if you're already in the Bairro Alto/Chiado.

During busy times, the long line (which wraps up the stairs and around behind the elevator's base) moves slowly. If it's backed up, skip it or come back at a quieter time. Two much faster routes up to Chiado are nearby: the elevators inside Armazéns do Chiado mall, or the escalators inside the Baixa-Chiado Metro station (see the sidebar on page 21).

Cost and Hours: Elevator and rooftop view deck-€5.15 (round-trip tickets only), view deck only-€1.50; elevator covered—without the deck—by 24-hour Viva Viagem card, or €1.30 with

António Salazar

Q: What do you get when you cross a lawyer, an economist, and a dictator?

A: António Salazar, who was all three—a dictator who ruled Portugal through harsh laws and a strict budget that hurt the poor.

Shortly after a 1926 military coup "saved" Portugal's floundering democracy from itself, General Oscar Carmona appointed António de Oliveira Salazar (1889-1970) as finance minister. A former professor of economics and law at the University of Coimbra, Salazar balanced the budget and the interests of the country's often-warring factions. His skill and his reputation as a clean-living, fair-minded patriot earned him a promotion. In 1932, he became prime minister, and he set about creating his New State (Estado Novo).

For nearly four decades, Salazar ruled a stable but isolated nation by harmonizing the traditional power blocs of the ruling class—the military, big business, large landowners, and the Catholic Church. He enforced his Christian fascism with the backing of the military—and his secret police.

As a person, Salazar was respected, but not loved. The son of a farm manager, he originally studied to be a priest before going on to become a scholar and writer. He never married. Quiet, low-key, and unassuming, he attended church regularly and lived a nonmaterialistic existence. But when faced with opposition, he was ruthless, and his secret police became an object of fear and hatred.

Salazar steered Portugal through the turmoil of Spain's Civil War (1936-1939), remaining officially neutral while secretly supporting Franco's fascists. He detested Nazi Germany's "pagan" leaders, but respected Mussolini for reconciling with the pope. In World War II, Portugal was officially neutral, but was often friendly with longtime ally Britain and used as a base for espionage. After the war, Salazar's regime benefited greatly from the United States' Marshall Plan for economic recovery (which Spain missed out on during Franco's rule). The country joined NATO in 1949.

Salazar distracted his poor and isolated masses with a cynical credo: "*Fado, Fátima, and Futebol!*" (the three "Fs"). Salazar was undone by two factors: the liberal 1960s and the unpopular, draining wars Portugal fought abroad to try to keep its colonial empire intact. When Salazar died in 1970, the regime that followed became increasingly less credible, leading to the liberating events of the Carnation Revolution in 1974 (see "The Carnation Revolution" sidebar, earlier).

zapping; departures every 10 minutes, daily 7:00-23:00, until 21:00 in winter.

▲Mouraria District

The Mouraria stretches steeply from Praça Martim Moniz up to the back side of São Jorge Castle. This historic tangled quarter was where Muslim Moors were banished after the Christian Reconquista of Lisbon in 1147. And 500 years later it is still the Muslim quarter—shared with other immigrant communities. Portugal's far-flung empire was given up in the last couple of generations; here in the old colonial capital you'll see people from Brazil, Goa, Mozambique, Angola, and many other former Portuguese outposts.

Visiting Mouraria: Young, edgy **Martim Moniz square** is the stage and living room of the roughly two dozen nationalities that call the Mouraria home: Many recent arrivals speak little or no Portuguese, and you'll even see stylized Arabic script in the Martim Moniz Metro station.

Two giant department stores, Centro Comercial Mouraria and Centro Comercial Martim Moniz—one Chinese owned and the other Indian owned—flank the square. Women in traditional colorful garments watch children dance while Goans play cricket. Meanwhile, in the "fusion market" on and around the square, entrepreneurs run small stalls with spicy and multiethnic foods. A long line of tourists wait to catch the #28E trolley, while unemployed people just hang out.

Near the trolley stop, an escalator carries people high into Mouraria. Beyond the escalator is the small **Chapel of Nossa Senhora da Saúde,** dedicated to Our Lady of Good Health, recalling an era when the Black Death killed millions; it's worth popping in to see its *azulejos* tiles (Rua da Mouraria 1). Look down at the unique *calçada* out front to find a full-scale outline of the chapel's facade by op art guru Eduardo Nery. This marks the start of the main street of the community: Rua da Mouraria.

At #90 on Rua da Mouraria, **Rua do Capelão** leads uphill into the back lanes of this world. Considered unsafe just a few years ago, it's now Lisbon's new happening spot.

The guitar monument at the intersection is a reminder that this is considered the birthplace of fado. Today, the lanes are decorated with black-and-white photos on walls (with English descriptions) marking homes of famous local fado musicians, noisy street art, and playgrounds just being fun.

There are plenty of inviting little eateries. For lunch, consider Zé da Mouraria (lunch only, Rua João Outeiro 24). It's an amazing scene. For a moveable feast, consider taking one of the popular Mouraria food tours (see "Tours in Lisbon," earlier).

The highest street, Rua das Farinhas, leads right to **Largo São**

Cristóvão. You could continue around toward the castle, past a former five-floor market, **Chão do Loureiro,** where each floor is a "gallery" filled with works by one of the country's top street artists (Calçada Marquês de Tancos 1). The top floor hides a café with a nice viewpoint. Or, from there, steps lead down past great street art to the edge of the Baixa (Rua da Madalena) and into the regular world once again.

NORTH LISBON

The main sight here is the Gulbenkian Museum, two miles north of the city center and just a few minutes' ride on the Metro blue line. A visit here can be combined with sightseeing in Belém, a quick taxi ride away.

▲▲Gulbenkian Museum (Museu Calouste Gulbenkian)

This is the best of Lisbon's 40 museums, and it's worth the trip for art lovers. This wide-ranging collection, with nothing Portuguese, spans 5,000 years of European, Egyptian, Islamic, and Asian art. It offers the most purely enjoyable museum-going experience in Iberia—it's both educational and just plain beautiful. The museum is cool, uncrowded, gorgeously lit, and easy to grasp, displaying only a few select and exquisite works from each epoch. Art Nouveau fans love the museum's stunning Lalique jewelry collection. Walk through five millennia of human history, appreciating our ancestors by seeing objects they treasured.

The museum is actually two museums—the main collection and the Gulbenkian Garden and Modern Collection (Coleção Moderna), a five-minute walk away through a delightful 18-acre lushly landscaped park. If walking from the main museum back to the Metro, the garden and Modern Collection are on the way (the museum's info desk has a handy map of the entire site).

Cost and Hours: €10, includes main branch and Modern Collection (located across park), free on Sun after 14:00; open Wed-Mon 10:00-18:00, closed Tue; Berna 45, +351 217 823 000, www.gulbenkian.pt.

Getting There: From downtown, hop a cab or take the Metro to the São Sebastião stop; leave the platform by following *Avenida de Aguiar (norte)* signs. Then, to leave the station, follow signs to *Avenida de Aguiar (nascente).* Once at street level, it's about a five-minute walk: Go a long block downhill on Avenida de Aguiar with the massive El Corte Inglés department store behind you. Just be-

Gulbenkian Museum

To Bullring

Gardens

❼

❹

ATRIUM ❻ ATRIUM

❾ ❺

❽ ❸

❷

❶

🔟

AVENIDA DE BERNA

POOL

POOL

⬆ ENTER

SIDEWALK

Not to Scale

OFFICE BLDG.

To Praça de Espanha

To Modern Collection, Avenida de Aguiar & S. Sebastião Metro Stop

❶ Egypt	❻ Renaissance & Baroque Painting
❷ Greece & Rome	❼ Louis XIV, XV & XVI
❸ Islamic World	❽ Romantic to Impressionist Paintings
❹ Far East	❾ René Lalique Jewelry
❺ Medieval Europe	🔟 Stairs down to WC & Café

fore the roundabout, you'll see a small sign pointing right to the *fundação*—the museum entrance is up the stairs and straight ahead through this park, past a long concrete office building, about 100 yards away.

Cuisine Art: Cafeterias are in both museum buildings, though I like the one in the Modern Collection building much better.

Background: Calouste Gulbenkian (1869-1955), an Armenian oil tycoon, gave Portugal his art collection (or "harem," as he called it) in gratitude for the hospitable asylum granted him in Lisbon during World War II (where he lived from 1942 until his death). The Portuguese consider Gulbenkian an inspirational model of how to be thoughtfully wealthy: He made a habit of "tithing for art," spending 10 percent of his income on things of beauty, and his billion-dollar estate is still a vital arts foundation promoting culture in Portugal.

In short, Gulbenkian had all the money in the world, dedicated much of his life to collecting what he thought was the most beautiful art anywhere, built this fine building to show it off, and left it as a gift to posterity.

Visiting the Museum: From the entrance lobby, there are two wings on one floor: roughly pre-1500 and post-1500. Following the museum's mostly chronological layout, you'll pass through the following sections:

❶ **Egypt** (2500-500 BC): If this room feels like a tomb, that's intentional. Everything here was once the personal property of

Egyptian kings and queens, including some pieces from King Tut—who died thinking you *can* take it with you. Ancient Egyptians, believing that life really began after death, carved statues to preserve the memory of the deceased, whether it be the head of a pharaoh carved out of "harder-than-stone" obsidian or a family pet. The cat statue nurses her kittens atop a coffin that once held the cat's mummy, preserved for the afterlife. Egyptians honored cats—even giving them gold earrings (notice this statue's ears are pierced). They believed cats helped the goddess Bastet keep watch over the household. Now, thousands of years later, we remember the Egyptians for these sturdy, dignified statues, built for eternity.

❷ **Greece and Rome** (500 BC-AD 500): The black-and-red Greek vase (calyx-crater), decorated with scenes of half-human satyrs chasing human women, reminds us of the rational Greeks' struggle to overcome their barbarian, animal-like urges as they invented Western civilization. Alexander the Great (r. 336-323 BC, seen on a series of gold medallions filling a glass case) used war to spread Greek culture throughout the Mediterranean, creating a cultural empire that would soon be taken over by Roman emperors. Gulbenkian loved collecting coins: The first treasure he acquired was a coin, purchased at age 11.

A carved stone on the wall near the exit brings you even further back in time to Mesopotamia (modern Iraq) and the very roots of civilization. The Assyrian relief of Ashurnasirpal II (884-859 BC) evokes this distant culture, which invented writing. Note the inscription chiseled over the portrait.

❸ Islamic World (700-1500): The Muslims who lived in Portugal—as far west of Mecca as you could get back then—might have decorated their homes with furnishings from all over the Islamic world. Imagine a Moorish sultan, dressed in a shirt from Syria, sitting on a carpet from Persia in a courtyard with Moroccan tiles. By a bubbling fountain, he puffs on a hookah.

Glazed and painted ceramics are from 13th-century Syria—specifically from the region in and around Raqqa (in the news recently as the capital of ISIS).

The intricate patterns on the Eygptian gilded and enameled glass lamps from a 14th-century mosque (behind the partition on the left) are not only beautiful...they're actually Arabic quotes from the Quran, such as "Allah is the light of the world, shining like a flame in a glass lamp, as bright as a star." Explore this large and rich collection, and then head a few thousand miles east.

The carpets you'll see were a passion for Gulbenkian (his family was long in the carpet trading business). He considered a carpet a garden you can bring inside your home.

❹ Far East (1368-1644): For almost 300 years, the Ming dynasty ruled China, having reclaimed the country from Genghis Khan and his sons. When Portuguese traders reached the Orient, they brought back blue-and-white ceramics such as these. They became all the rage, inspiring the creation of both Portuguese tiles and Dutch Delftware. Writing utensils fill elaborately decorated boxes from Japan. Another type of box—a Japanese *bento*—was the ultimate picnic basket, perfect for an excursion to the Japanese countryside.

Crossing into the next wing, you enter the section on European art.

❺ Medieval Europe (500-1500): While China was thriving and inventing, Europe was stuck in a thousand-year medieval funk (with the exception of Muslim Arab-ruled Iberia). Most Europeans from the "Age of Faith" channeled their spirituality into objects of Christian devotion. A priest on a business trip could pack a portable, collapsible altarpiece in his backpack, travel to a remote village that had no church, and deliver a sermon illustrated by scenes carved in ivory. In monasteries, the monks with the best penmanship laboriously copied books (illuminated manuscripts) and decorated them with scenes from the text—and left wacky doodles in the margins. These books are virtual time capsules, preserving the knowledge of Greece and Rome until it could emerge again, a thousand years later, in the Renaissance.

❻ Renaissance and Baroque Painting (1500-1700): Around 1500, a cultural revolution was taking place—the birth of humanism. Painters saw God in the faces of ordinary people, whether in Domenico Ghirlandaio's fresh-faced maiden, Frans Hals' wrinkled old woman, or Rembrandt's portrait of an old man, whose crease-lined hands tell the story of his life. Also in this section are exquisite works by Van der Weyden, Van Dyck, and Rubens.

Propelled by the Italian-born Renaissance, Europe's focus shifted northward to the luxurious court of France, where a new secular culture was blossoming—as illustrated in sumptuous tapestries. The three-part series *Playing Children* (c. 1540) features Fishing, the Dance, and the Ball Game.

❼ **Louis XIV, XV, XVI** (1700-1800): This furniture, once owned by French kings (and Marie-Antoinette and Madame de Pompadour), is a royal home show. Anything heavy, ornate, and gilded (or that includes curved legs and animal-clawed feet) is from the time of Louis XIV. The Louis XV style is lighter and daintier, with Asian motifs, while furniture from the Louis XVI era is stripped-down, straight-legged, tapered, and more modern.

❽ **Romantic to Impressionist Paintings** (1700-2000): Europe ruled the world, and art became increasingly refined. Young British aristocrats (Thomas Gainsborough portrait) traveled Europe on the Grand Tour to see great sights like Venice. They would take home small, photo-realistic Venicescapes—such as an entire room of Guardi landscapes (c. 1780)—as souvenirs.

Follow the progression in styles from stormy Romanticism (J. M. W. Turner's tumultuous shipwreck) to Realism's breath-of-fresh-air simplicity (Manet's bubble-blower, Degas' portraits) to the glinting, shimmering Impressionism of Monet and Renoir. Statues by Rodin are Impressionism in stone.

❾ **René Lalique Jewelry:** Finish your visit with the stunning, sumptuous Art Nouveau glasswork and jewelry of French designer René Lalique (1860-1945). Fragile beauty like this, from the elegant turn-of-the-century belle époque, was about to be shattered by the turbulent 20th century. Art Nouveau borrowed forms from nature and valued the organic and artisanal over the mass-produced. Ordinary dragonflies, orchids, and

beetles become breathtaking when transformed into jewelry. Sarah Bernhardt wore Lalique—art you hang not on a wall, but on your body. The work of Lalique—just another of Gulbenkian's circle of friends—is a fitting finale to this museum of history and beauty.

Modern Collection and Garden: Stimulating if you like contemporary and abstract art, the Modern Collection's temporary exhibits offer a fun bit of whimsy if you have the energy and inclination. The classy modern building is set in a delightful garden—a favorite for locals enjoying a quiet or romantic moment—and often hosts classical music concerts in its auditoriums.

WEST LISBON

The Museum of Ancient Art, west of downtown, is halfway to Belém and can be combined with an excursion there.

▲▲Museum of Ancient Art (Museu Nacional de Arte Antiga)

Not "ancient" as in Roman and Greek—but "antique" as in Age of Discovery—this is Portugal's finest museum for artwork from the time when the Portuguese ruled the seas: the 15th and 16th centuries. (Most of these works were gathered from Lisbon's abbeys and convents after their dissolution in 1834.) You'll also find a rich collection of furniture, as well as paintings by renowned European masters such as Hieronymus Bosch, Jan van Eyck, and Raphael—all in a grand palace that's sleekly renovated and well-presented.

Cost and Hours: €6, Tue-Sun 10:00-18:00, closed Mon; good cafeteria with shaded garden seating overlooking the river, Rua das Janeles Verdes 9, +351 213 912 800, www.museudearteantiga.pt.

Getting There: It's about a mile west of downtown Lisbon. From Praça da Figueira, take trolley #15E to Cais Rocha, cross the street, and walk up a lot of steps. To stop right in front, take bus #714 from either Praça da Figueira or Praça do Comércio. Note that trolley #15E and bus #714 both continue to the sights in Belém; consider stopping here at the end of your Belém day.

Visiting the Museum: Here are some of the museum's highlights, starting on the top floor. From the ticket desk, turn right to find the elevator and press button 3.

Top Floor, Portuguese Painting and Sculpture: From the elevator, veer right through the atrium and find the big, red room at the far end. *The Panels of St. Vincent* are a multipart altarpiece by the late-15th-century master Nuno Gonçalves. A gang of 60 real people—everyone from royalty to sailors and beggars—surrounds Lisbon's patron saint. Of note is the only recognized portrait of Prince Henry the Navigator, responsible for setting Portugal on the path to exploration. Find him on the third panel—an elder gentleman dressed in black with a wide-brimmed hat, hands together almost in prayer. Other masterworks by Gonçalves, painted just before the Age of Discovery, hang behind the panels. Also of note is a small but lifelike portrait of King João I, with hands clasped in prayer, by an unknown artist. This is the very first painting ever of a Portuguese monarch, winner of the Batalha battle and founder of a new dynasty.

Explore the rest of the floor clockwise from the panels: Opposite the panels, find an exceptional portrait of the baby-faced King Sebastian—who died young when he led an incursion into Africa. The armor is typical of Iberia for the era, as is the royal jaw and pursed lips caused by inbreeding with many generations of Habsburgs from Spain. If you've visited the sights in Belém, you'll recognize the Monastery of Jerónimos before it was fully decorated (1657 painting by Felipe Lobo).

Before you head down the stairs (in the middle of the atrium) to the next floor, notice the statue of a pregnant Mary *(The Virgin of Expectation,* c. 1340-1350). This unusual theme was common in rural parts of Portugal (such as the Alentejo, the close-to-the-ground region in the southeast), where the Virgin's fertility was her most persuasive quality in recruiting local followers.

Middle Floor, Art from the Portuguese Discoveries: This floor collects items that Portuguese explorers brought home from their far-flung travels. Coming down the stairs, bear left, then right, to find the room with four large, enchanting Namban screen paintings *(Namban,* meaning "southern barbarians," the catch-all term the Japanese applied to all foreigners). These show the Portuguese from a 16th-century Japanese perspective—with long noses, dark complexions, and great skill at climbing rigging, like acrobats. The Portuguese, the first Europeans to make contact with Japan,

gave the Japanese guns, Catholicism (Nagasaki was founded by Portuguese Jesuits), and a new deep-frying technique we now know as tempura.

Now exit right and do a counterclockwise circle around this floor, stocked with furniture, large vases, ivory carvings, fine china, and ceramics. Imagine how astonishing these treasures must have seemed when the early explorers returned with them. Facing the atrium are some beautiful tiles from Damascus—a gift from Calouste Gulbenkian (founder of the Gulbenkian Museum). After a lot of ceramics, eventually you reach a treasury of gold and silver items. Look for the freestanding glass case with a gorgeous golden monstrance, with its carrying case displayed just behind it—the bejeweled Rococo Communion-host holder was made for Lisbon's Bemposta Palace. Farther along is the smaller yet even more exquisite Monstrance of Belém, commissioned by Manuel I and made from East African tribute gold brought back by Vasco da Gama. Squint at the fine enamel creatures filling a tide pool on the base, the 12 apostles gathered around the glass case for the Communion wafer (the fancy top pops off), and the white dove hanging like a mobile under the all-powerful God bidding us peace on earth.

Heading back to the atrium, don't miss the small, dimly lit room (on the left) displaying an impressive jewelry collection, including pieces decorated with the red cross of the affluent Order of Christ, whose members helped plan and fund Portuguese explorations.

Back in the atrium, before continuing downstairs, stop to admire a 17th-century painting of Lisbon before the 1755 earthquake. Notice the royal palace on Praça do Comércio, the shipyards next to the royal palace (now a public park), and the ship-clogged Rio Tejo.

Ground Floor, European Paintings: Pass through the gift shop, veer left, and follow the one-way route through paintings from all over Europe. A few rooms in, note the larger-than-life paintings of the 12 apostles by the Spanish master Zurburán. Continue to the end of the hall, then loop back around to find the room with Bosch's *Temptations of St. Anthony* (a three-paneled altarpiece fantasy, c. 1500) and Albrecht Dürer's *St. Jerome*. St. Jerome— you'll see other portraits of him in this collection, always with a skull—is all-important to Lisbon as the primary figure behind the Monastery of Jerónimos in Belém. Finally, wander through the few remnants of the palace. Note the Pombal coat-of-arms that decorates the elaborate, Baroque doorway at the top of the staircase (find the star); the palace was originally purchased by the brother of the powerful Marquês de Pombal. Take a well-earned break at the museum cafeteria. Sit outside in the gardens, with wonderful river views, and watch all the boats go by.

BELÉM DISTRICT

About five miles west of downtown Lisbon, the Belém district is a stately pincushion of important sights from Portugal's Golden Age, when Vasco da Gama and company turned the country into Europe's wealthiest power. Belém was the sending-off point for voyages in the Age of Discovery. Before embarking, sailors would stay and pray at the Monastery of Jerónimos, and when they returned, the Belém Tower welcomed them home. The grand buildings of

Belém survived the great 1755 earthquake, so this is the best place to experience the Manueline architectural style (for more on this style, see the sidebar on page 78). After the earthquake, safety-conscious (and rattled) royalty chose to live uphill from here—in tents rather than stone buildings. The modern-day president of Portugal calls Belém home.

To celebrate a double anniversary (800 years since the founding of Portugal and 300 years of independence from Spain), a grand exhibition was held here in 1940, resulting in fine parks, fountains, and monuments.

Getting to Belém: You have multiple options. By **taxi** or **Uber,** figure no more than about 20 minutes and €10 from downtown. **Buses** #714 and #728 serve Belém, and the coastal train line running from Lisbon's **Cais do Sodré station** gets you there in about 10 minutes.

When I have the time, I prefer riding the slower **trolley** #15E (30 minutes, catch at Praça da Figueira or Praça do Comércio). In Belém, the first trolley stop is at the National Coach Museum (stop is called simply "Belém"—you'll see the brown sign for *Museu dos Coches* just before the stop); the second stop (Belém-Jerónimos) is at the Monastery of Jerónimos (it's huge—you can't miss it); and another (Pedrouços) is two stops farther, at a little square two blocks inland from the Belém Tower.

Eateries
1 Rest. Os Jerónimos & Casa Pastéis de Belém
2 A Padaria Portuguesa
3 Floresta de Belém & Queijadas de Belém
4 Gelados Santini

Planning Your Time: Nearly all of Belém's museums are closed on Monday (though the Monument to the Discoveries is open Mon May-Sept). Consider doing Belém's sights from east to west, in the order you'll reach them from the tram or train: the National Coach Museum, pastry and coffee break, Monastery of Jerónimos, Maritime Museum and/or lunch at its cafeteria (public access, museum entry not required), Monument to the Discoveries, and Belém Tower. If arriving by taxi, you could start at Belém Tower—the farthest point—and do the recommended lineup in reverse, ending at the National Coach Museum (which has easier public transit connections than the tower). Belém also has a cultural center, a children's museum, and a planetarium—not priorities for a quick visit. While walking between sights, be aware that train tracks to Cascais cut off access to the riverside from inland museums. Three pedestrian passes (an overpass at the Coach Museum, an underpass at the Monument to the Discoveries, and another overpass near Belém Tower) are the only ways to cross over. For recommended eateries in this area, see the sidebar in this section.

Crowd-Beating Tips: Belém's sights are often crowded in the morning. In peak season, there can be long lines at the Belém Tower and at the monastery. If there is a line at the tower, I simply wouldn't go in. There's almost nothing inside to see (though the view is nice). At the monastery, crowds usually diminish after 16:00.

Returning to Downtown: When you're through, hop on trolley #15E or bus #714 to return to Praça da Figueira or Praça do Comércio, or ride the coastal train back to Cais do Sodré. Note that there are two different end stops for the #15E listed clearly on the front of the tram: Praça da Figueira or Cais do Sodré; both take you to the city center. If you have time and energy left, you could hop off the trolley or bus to tour the Museum of Ancient Art on the way home. Bus #728 takes you to Santa Apolónia station, and continues to Parque das Nações and Oriente station.

Tourist Information: A little TI kiosk is directly across the street from the entrance to the monastery. They sell monastery tickets as well as the LisboaCard (sporadic hours but usually open Tue-Sat 10:00-13:00 & 14:00-18:00, closed Sun-Mon, +351 213 658 437).

▲▲National Coach Museum (Museu Nacional dos Coches)

In 1905, the last queen of Portugal saw that cars would soon obliterate horse-drawn carriages as a form of transportation. She decided to preserve her fine collection of royal coaches, which became today's National Coach Museum. The impressive collection is split between two buildings, each with its own ticket. The main branch—in a huge, blocky, concrete building closer to the river—has the bulk of the collection, with 70 dazzling coaches, all described in English. The Royal Riding School, closer to the trolley tracks, is a historical space with a gorgeous interior but only about 10 coaches on display. If you want to really appreciate the coaches themselves, focus on the main branch. But to see regal spaces (which are rare in Lisbon), add on the Royal Riding School.

Cost and Hours: Main branch-€8, Royal Riding School-€4, €10 combo-ticket covers both, open Tue-Sun 10:00-17:00, closed Mon, +351 213 610 850, www.museudoscoches.pt.

Visiting the Main Branch: The museum is right across the street from the Belém tram stop (on one side) and the Belém train station (on the other). Find the ticket office under the building (opposite the museum entrance), then ride an elevator or take steps up to the collection, where you'll loop through two long rooms.

The first coach dates from around 1600. This crude and simple vehicle was once used by Philip II, king of Spain and Portugal, to shuttle between Madrid and Lisbon. Notice that the coach has no driver's seat—its drivers would actually ride the horses. You'll have to trust me on this, but if you lift up the cushion from the passengers' seat, you'll find a potty hole—also handy for road sickness. Imagine how slow and rough the ride would be with bad roads and a crude leather-strap suspension.

From here, walk through the historical collection, displayed chronologically. Study the evolution of suspension technology, made in the 15th century in the Hungarian town of Kocs (pronounced "coach"—hence the name). By the 17th century—when this collection begins—coaches had caught on in a big way in Portugal, which was an early adopter. Trace the improvements made through the next century, noticing that as the decoration increases, so does the comfort. A Portuguese coat of arms indicates that a carriage was part of the royal fleet. Ornamentation often includes a folk festival of exotic faces from Portugal's distant colonies.

In the middle of the hall shines the lumbering Oceans Coach, as ornate as it is long. At the stern, gold figures symbolize the Atlantic and Indian Oceans holding hands, a reminder of Portugal's mastery of the sea. The Oceans Coach is flanked by two equally stunning coaches with similar symbols of ocean exploration. These were part of a thematic convoy sent by King João V to Pope Clement XI in 1716.

Next you'll see a pair of carriages from the royal couple ruling Portugal when the 1755 earthquake struck. King José I rode in a sumptuously carved Baroque masterpiece while Queen Mariana Victoria opted for a more subdued ride. At the far end of the hall, peek inside the Table coach, which must have been a cozy place to hang out and wait for the exchange.

In the next room, you'll mainly see "Berlins"—a new coach type (pioneered in that city, in the late 17th century) that suspended the main compartment on thick leather straps to improve the ride. You'll see ecclesiastical coaches (suggesting the high status of clergy); single-horse chaise and cabriolet coaches (including some sleek, black leather, 19th-century, Sherlock Holmes-style ones); hunting vehicles; sedan chairs; scaled-down play carriages for kids who had everything; and mail coaches. You may see the "Landau of the Regicide"—the coach in which King Carlos I and his heir were shot and killed on February 1, 1908. You can still see the bullet holes. (This carriage is often out on loan.)

Royal Riding School: You'll find this regal building along the trolley tracks through Belém, kitty-corner from the main museum. The elegant old riding room with its dramatically painted ceiling is as remarkable as the carriages. Under that ceiling, you'll see a handful of fine specimens (but if you've already been to the main branch, this is a rerun). Firefighters will appreciate the second

Eating in Belém

You'll find snack bars at Belém Tower, a cafeteria at the Maritime Museum, and fun little restaurants along Rua de Belém, between the National Coach Museum and the monastery. Here are a few other eateries worth checking out:

$$ Restaurante Os Jerónimos: Popular for fresh fish, this is where hardworking Carlos treats his customers well and serves fine, affordable meals and a fish-of-the-day special (Sun-Fri 12:00-21:30, closed Sat, Rua de Belém 74, +351 213 638 423, next to renowned Casa Pastéis de Belém pastry café).

$ A Padaria Portuguesa: This respected chain bakery has fine fresh-baked bread, hearty sandwiches, and salads (daily 7:30-20:00, Rua de Belém 46).

$$ Restaurant Row Options: Many more fine places with outdoor seating are in the restaurant row beyond the McDonald's facing the park, including **Floresta de Belém,** the local favorite for their home-style Portuguese cooking, such as tasty grilled sardines and *feijoada* bean stew. They have minimal seating inside, but two cozy terraces outside (closed Sun dinner, all day Mon, and Sept; Praça Afonso de Albuquerque 1A, +351 213 636 307). Next door, **Queijadas de Belém** is a good bet for its salads, sardines, and outside seating (daily, Rua de Belém 1, +351 213 630 034).

Dessert: In addition to the original *pastel de Belém* place (**Casa Pastéis de Belém,** described below), **Gelados Santini**—a local favorite for gelato—is near the entrance to the National Coach Museum.

room, displaying a history of horse-drawn vehicles used to put out Lisbon blazes.

Nearby: Just past the Royal Riding School, on the landscaped hill behind the wall, is the stately, pink **Belém Palace**—the residence of Portugal's president. The palace interior is tourable only on Saturdays (€5, most tours in Portuguese), but if you're fascinated by Portuguese history, you can drop in anytime at the modern little **Museum of the Portuguese Presidents** (Museu da Presidência da República). It offers a little lesson on each of Portugal's democracy-era presidents (since 1910) and lots of state gifts (€2.50, Tue-Sun 10:00-18:00, closed Mon, look for entrance just west of Royal Riding School and palace gate).

▲Casa Pastéis de Belém

This café is the birthplace of the wonderful custard tart that's called *pastel de nata* throughout Portugal, but here it's dubbed *pastel de Belém*. You can explore this sprawling temple to Portugal's beloved custard tart like a museum, with a peek at the bakery in the rear.

Since 1837, residents have been coming to this café to get their tarts fresh. Its popularity stems mainly from the fact that their recipe is a closely guarded secret—supposedly only three people know the exact proportions of the ingredients. While the recipe is fine, my hunch is that their undeniable goodness is simply because the café cranks out 20,000 or so a day—you get them fresh and crunchy, literally hot out of the oven. (Take one back to your hotel and eat it tonight and it'll taste just like any other in town.) Sit down and enjoy one with a *café com leite*. Sprinkle on as much cinnamon and powdered sugar as you like.

LISBON

Tarts are €1.10 whether you eat in or carry out. There are two separate lines for take-away; both move quickly (pay, then bring receipt to counter to claim your tart). If the lines are extremely long, table service inside the café may be faster (daily 8:00-23:00, Rua de Belém 84, +351 213 637 423).

▲▲▲Monastery of Jerónimos (Mosteiro dos Jerónimos)

This giant, white limestone church and monastery stretches for 300 impressive yards along the Belém waterfront. It was built over a hundred years and is ba-

sically a Gothic structure with Manueline ornamentation. King Manuel (who ruled from 1495) erected it as a "thank you" for the discoveries made by early Portuguese explorers (Vasco da Gama's tomb is inside). This is a "Pepper Monument," financed in part with "pepper money," a 5 percent tax on spices brought back from India. Manuel built the church near the site of a humble chapel where sailors spent their last night ashore in prayer before embarking on frightening voyages.

Cost and Hours: Church-free, cloister-€10, €12 combo-ticket with Archaeology Museum; monastery open Tue-Sun 10:00-18:30, Oct-April until 17:30, closed Mon year-round; www.mosteirojeronimos.pt.

Getting In: Buy your monastery ticket at the Archaeology Museum (to the left of the monastery) or at the TI kiosk in the park across the street. Note that LisboaCard holders must get a voucher (from either the Archaeology Museum ticket office or the TI kiosk) before heading to the monastery. At the monastery, you'll see two lines. The fast-moving right queue is for the church (free to enter); the line on the left is for the cloister.

Background: As you circle around the complex, ponder the great history of this serene place. Monks often accompanied the

Monastery of Jerónimos

- ← PESSOA TOMB
- REFECTORY
- FOUNTAIN
- CLOISTER
- CHAPTER HOUSE
- SACRISTY
- CONFESSIONALS
- CONFESSIONALS
- CHURCH
- ELEPHANT TOMBS
- ENTRANCE
- To Archaeology Museum (monastery tickets) & Maritime Museum
- To National Coach Museum & Belém Station
- Praça do Império
- #15E (From Lisbon)
- Jardim da Praça do Império
- To Monument to the Discoveries

❶ South Portal
❷ Church Entrance
❸ Church Interior
❹ Memorial to Luís de Camões
❺ Renaissance Altar
❻ Tomb of Vasco da Gama
❼ Cloister Entrance
❽ Stairs Up to Bookshop & Choir

sailor-pirates on their trading/pillaging trips, hoping to convert the heathens to Christianity. Many expeditions were financed by the Order of Christ, a brotherhood of soldier-monks. The monks who inhabited this cloister were Hieronymites—followers of St. Jerome, hence the monastery name of Jerónimos. (You'll see several paintings of St. Jerome, living in a Holy Land desert in the fourth century, doing what he was best known for: translating the Bible into the Church's official Latin version.)

King Manuel, who did so much to promote exploration, was also the man who forcibly expelled all Jews from the country. (In 1497, the Spanish *Reyes Católicos*—Ferdinand and Isabel—allowed him to marry one of their daughters on the condition that he deport the Jews.) It was a time of extreme Christian faith. The sheer size of this religious complex is a testament to the religious motivation that—along with money—propelled the Age of Discovery.

➜ Self-Guided Tour: Start outside the monastery:

❶ South Portal: The fancy portal, facing the street, is text-book Manueline. Henry the Navigator stands between the doors with the king's patron saint, St. Jerome (above on the left, with the lion). Henry (Manuel's uncle) built the original sailors' chapel on this site. This door is only used when Mass lets out or for Saturday weddings. (The electronic snapping sound you hear is designed to keep the pigeons away.)

• *To the left of the portal is the...*

❷ Church Entrance: As you approach the main entrance, the church is on your right and the cloister is straight ahead. Flanking the church door are kneeling statues of King Manuel I, the Fortunate (left of door, with St. Jerome), and his second Spanish wife, María (right, with John the Baptist).

❸ Church Interior: The Manueline style is on the cusp of the Renaissance. The space is more open than earlier medieval

churches. Slender, palm-tree-like columns don't break the interior space (as Gothic columns would), and the ceiling is all one height. Motifs from the sea hide in the decor. The sea brought Portugal 16th-century wealth and power, making this art possible. You'll see rope-like arches, ships, and monsters that evoke

the mystery of undiscovered lands. Artichokes, eaten for their vitamin C to fend off scurvy, recall the hardships sailors faced at sea. Thankfully, except for the stained glass (which is 20th century), the church survived the 1755 quake.

• *On your right as you face the altar is the...*

❹ Memorial to Luís de Camões: Camões (kah-MOISH, 1524-1580) is Portugal's Shakespeare and Casanova rolled into one, an adventurer and writer whose heroic poems, glorifying the nation's sailing exploits, capture the spirit of the Portuguese people. It was Camões who described Portugal as the place "where land ends and the sea begins."

After college at Coimbra, Camões was banished from the court (1546) for flirting with the noble lady Dona Caterina. He lost an eye soldiering in Morocco (he's always portrayed squinting), served jail time for brawling with a bureaucrat, and then caught a ship to India and China, surviving a shipwreck on the way. While serving as a colonial administrator in India, he plugged away at the epic poem that would become his masterpiece. Returning to Portugal, he published *The Lusiads* (*Os Lusíadas*, 1572), winning minor recognition and a small pension.

The long poem describes Vasco da Gama's first voyage to India in heroic terms, on the scale of Homer's *Odyssey*. *The Lusiads* begins:

> *Arms and the heroes, from Lisbon's shore,*
> *sailed through seas never dared before,*
> *with awesome courage, forging their way*
> *to the glorious kingdoms of the rising day.*

The poem goes on to recite many events in Portuguese history, from the time of the Lusiads (the original pre-Roman natives) onward. Even today, Camões' words are quoted by modern Portuguese politicians in search of a heroic sound bite. And Portugal's national holiday, June 10, is known as Camões Day, remembering the day in 1580 when the great poet died. The stone monument here—with literary rather than maritime motifs—is an empty tomb (his actual burial spot is unknown).

• *Now head up to the front of the church, and the...*

❺ Renaissance Altar: This is a rare, pre-1755 interior in Lisbon (except for the stained glass, which is from 1940). Here, under the 90-foot wide towering main vault, are buried the royals of 16th-century Portugal. In the niches surrounding the main altar, elephants—a Far Eastern symbol of power, more powerful and kingly than the lion—support two kings and two queens (King Manuel I is front-left). Like many Portuguese churches (such as the cathedrals in downtown Lisbon and Évora), this was renovated in Renaissance and Baroque times, resulting in an odd mix of dark, older naves and pretty pastel altars.

Skip the **sacristy** (entrance in the corner), a single-columned room wrapped in paintings on wood featuring scenes from the life of St. Jerome (not worth the admission fee). Instead, do an about-face and head up the aisle on the right, back toward the entrance (noticing more elephants in the transept). You'll pass **seven wooden confessional doors** (on your right). Notice the ornamental carving around the second one: a festival of faces from newly encountered corners of the world. Head back toward the entry.

• *Under a ceiling that's a veritable Boy Scout's Handbook of rope and knots is the...*

❻ Tomb of Vasco da Gama: On the night of July 7, 1497, in the small chapel that once stood here, da Gama (1460-1524) prayed for a safe voyage. The next day, he set sail from Belém with four ships (see the caravel carved in the middle of the tomb's side) and 150 men. He was armed with state-of-the-art maps and sailing technology, such as the carved armillary sphere (to the right of the caravel)— a globe surrounded by movable rings designed to determine the positions of the sun or other stars to help sailors track their location on earth. (Some say its diagonal slash is sym-

bolic of the unwritten pact and ambition of Spain and Portugal to split the world evenly, but it actually represents the zodiac—the path of the planets as they move across the heavens.)

Da Gama's mission? To confirm what earlier navigators had hypothesized—that the ocean recently discovered when Bartolomeu Dias rounded Africa's Cape of Good Hope was the same one seen by overland travelers to India. Hopefully, da Gama would find a direct sea route to the vast, untapped wealth of Asia. The symbols on the tomb show the icons of the period—the cross (symbolizing the religious military order of the soldier-monks who funded these voyages), the caravel (representing the method of travel), and Portugal's trading power around the globe (the result).

By Christmas, da Gama rounded the Cape of Good Hope. After battling hostile Arabs in Mozambique, he hired an Arab guide to pilot the ships to India, arriving on the southwest coast in Calicut (from which we get the word "calico") in May 1498. He traded for spices, networked with the locals for future outposts, battled belligerent chiefs, and then headed back home. Da Gama and his crew arrived home to Lisbon in September 1499 (after two years and two months on the seas) and were greeted with all-out Vasco-mania. The few spices he'd returned with (many were lost in transit) were worth a staggering fortune. Portugal's Golden Age was launched.

King Manuel dubbed da Gama "Admiral of the Sea of India" and sent him out again, this time to subdue the Indian people, establish more trade outposts, and again return home to wealth and honor. Da Gama died on Christmas Eve 1524, in India. His memory lives on due to the tribute of two men: Manuel, who built this large church, and Luís de Camões (honored opposite Vasco), who turned da Gama's history-making voyage into an epic poem.

Before leaving, enjoy the big picture from a 500-years-ago perspective. It's the full package for Portugal: the country's finest church containing the great poet, the great explorer, and the royal family.

• *Leave the church, turn right, show your monastery ticket, and enter the...*

Manueline Architecture, c. 1480-1580

Portugal's unique decorative style (from its peak of power under King Manuel I, the Fortunate, r. 1495-1521) reflects the wealth of the times and the many cultural influences of the Age of Discovery. It is more an ornamental than structural style, blending late Gothic features with Mudejar (Moorish) elements. Craftsmen applied it equally to buildings with pointed Gothic or rounded Renaissance arches; you'll see elaborate Manueline carved stonework particularly around windows and doors.

The Manueline aesthetic is ornate, elaborate, and intertwined, often featuring symbols from a family's coat of arms (shields with castles, crosses, lions, banners, and crowns) or motifs from the sea (rope-like columns or borders, knots, shells, coral, anchors, and nets). Manuel's personal symbol was the armillary sphere—a celestial globe—which was an indispensable navigational aid for sailors. You'll also see imports of the age, from opium poppies to exotic animals.

Architecture students will recognize elements from Gothic's elaborate tracery, the abstract designs of Moorish culture, similarities to Spain's intricate Plateresque style (which dates from the same time), and the elongated excesses of Italian Mannerism.

❼ Cloister: This restored cloister is the architectural highlight of Belém. The lacy arcade is Manueline; the simpler diamond and decorative rose frieze above the top floor is Renaissance. Study the carvings, especially the gargoyles above the lower set of arches. Among these functioning rainspouts, find a monkey, a kitten, and a cricket.

Heads of state are often received in the cloister with a warm welcome. This is also the site of many important treaty signings, such as Portugal's admittance to the European Union in 1986. Turn left and do a clockwise spin around this fine space.

In the first corner, a small lion-topped basin (where the monks washed up before meals) marks the entrance to the **refectory**, or dining hall—today an occasional concert venue—lined with fine 18th-century tiles. The tiles are considered textbook Rococo, which ignores the parameters set by the architecture (unlike Baroque, which works within the structure).

Down the next stretch of cloister, on the left, is the burial spot of Portugal's most revered modern poet, **Fernando Pessoa** (see sidebar on page 54).

Continuing around, the former **chapter house** contains an exhibit of the lengthy restoration process, as well as the tomb of Alexandre Herculano, a Romantic 19th-century historian and poet. Quotes from Herculano adorn his tomb: "Sleep? Only the cold cadaver that doesn't feel sleeps. The soul flies and wraps itself around the feet of the All-Powerful."

• *Continuing around the cloister, find the stairs and head up.*

❽ **Upstairs:** At the top of the stairs, on the left, step into the Upper Choir (above the main door)—peering down into the vast sanctuary, at the feet of a powerful crucifix.

Back out in the upper cloister, circle around to find a bookshop (and the exit). All the way around are great cloister views. At the far end of the cloister is an exhibition that juxtaposes the historical timeline of this monastery and Portugal with contemporaneous world events (but no real artifacts).

▲Maritime Museum (Museu de Marinha)

If you're interested in Portugal's historic ships and navigational tools, this museum, which fills the west wing of the Monastery of Jerónimos (listed above), is worth a look. It's refreshingly uncrowded, and sailors love it.

Cost and Hours: €6.50, daily 10:00-18:00, Oct-April until 17:00, ccm.marinha.pt. It's at the far end of the long monastery building, facing the planetarium; the museum entrance is to your right, and its good **$$** cafeteria (open to the public) is to your left.

Visiting the Museum: You'll enter past huge statues of great explorers, then follow the one-way route (with English explanations) through the sprawling collection, offering a well-presented recap of an age when Portugal ruled the waves. It's loaded with artifacts and reproductions: nautical paintings, model ships, cannons, uniforms, and maps illustrating Portuguese explorations. The exhibit takes you right up to the present day, covering not just explorers and military vessels but also the fishing industry. You'll see the reconstructed king's and queen's staterooms from aboard King Carlos I's royal yacht *Amélia*. Then you'll walk outside (under a connecting gallery) to reach a vast warehouse of actual boats—from rustic *rabelos* to yawls to ceremonial royal barges. The centerpiece is the massive barge of King João VI, with 38 oars pulled by some 80 oarsmen, and plush royal quarters at the stern.

▲Monument to the Discoveries (Padrão dos Descobrimentos)

In 1960, the city honored the 500th anniversary of the death of Prince Henry the Navigator by rebuilding this giant riverside

monument, which had originally been constructed for a 1940 world's fair. It takes the shape of a huge caravel ship, in full sail, with Henry at the helm and the great navigators, sailors, and explorers on board behind him. The elevator inside takes you up to the tiptop for a tingly vista— including a fine aerial view down over the mural in front.

Cost and Hours: €5; daily 10:00-19:00; Oct-April Tue-Sun until 18:00, closed Mon; +351 213 031 950, www.padraodosdescobrimentos.pt.

Visiting the Monument: To get here, find the pedestrian tunnel under the busy boulevard, then walk around the huge monument. The 170-foot concrete structure shows that exploring the world was a team effort. The men who braved the unknown stand on the pointed, raised prow of a caravel, about to be launched into the Rio Tejo.

Leading the charge is Prince Henry the Navigator, holding a model of a caravel and a map, followed by kneeling kings and soldiers who Christianized foreign lands with the sword. Behind Henry (on the west side, away from bridge), find the men who financed the voyages (King Manuel I, holding an armillary sphere, his personal symbol), those who glorified it in poems and paintings (like Luís de Camões, holding his famous poem *The Lusiads* on a scroll), and at the very end, the only woman, Philippa of Lancaster, Henry's British mother.

On the east side (closest to bridge—as you walk, notice the optical illusion of waves on the flat cobbled surface), Vasco da Gama stands with his eyes on the horizon and his hand on his sword. Magellan holds a circle, representing the round earth his ship circumnavigated, while in front of him, Pedro Cabral puts

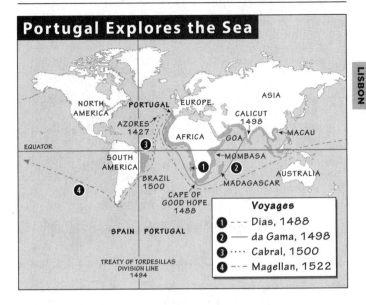

Portugal Explores the Sea

Voyages

1 - - - Dias, 1488
2 —— da Gama, 1498
3 ···· Cabral, 1500
4 - - - Magellan, 1522

his hand to his heart, thankful to have (perhaps accidentally) arrived in Brazil. Various monks, navigators with maps, and crusaders with flags complete the crew. Check out the pillory, decorated with the Portuguese coat of arms and a cross, erected in each place "discovered" by the Portuguese—leaving no doubt as to which Europeans had arrived first.

In the **marble map in the pavement** (a gift from South Africa) in front of the Monument to the Discoveries, follow Portugal's explorers as they inched out into monster-infested waters at the edge of the world. From their tiny, isolated nation in Europe, the Portuguese first headed south to the coast of Morocco, conquering the Muslims of Ceuta in God's name (1415) and trying to gain control of North African trade routes. They braved the open Atlantic to the west and southwest, stumbling on the Madeiras (1420), which Prince Henry planted with vineyards, and the remote Azore Islands (Açores, 1427).

Meanwhile, the Portuguese slowly moved southward, hugging the African coast, each voyage building on the knowledge from previous expeditions. They cleared the biggest psychological hump when Gil Eanes sailed around Cape Bojador (western Sahara, 1434)—the border of the known world—and into the equatorial seas where it was thought that sea monsters lurked, no winds blew, and ships would be incinerated in the hot sun. Eanes survived, returning home with 200 enslaved Africans, the first of what would become a lucrative, abhorrent commodity. Two generations later, Bartolomeu Dias rounded the southern tip of Africa (Cabo da Boa Esperança,

Caravels

These easily maneuverable trading ships were fast, small (80 feet), and light (100 tons), with few guns and three triangular-shaped sails (called lateen-rigged sails) that could pivot quickly to catch the wind. They were ideal for sailing along coastlines. Many ocean-going caravels were also rigged with a square foresail for stability. (This photo shows the model held by Prince Henry on Belém's Monument to the Discoveries.) Columbus' *Niña* and *Pinta* were rerigged caravels.

1488), discovering the sea route to Asia that Vasco da Gama (1498) and others would exploit to establish trade and outposts in India, Indonesia, Japan, and China (Macao in 1557, on the south coast).

In 1500, Pedro Cabral (along with Dias and 1,200 men) took a wi-i-i-ide right turn on the way down the African coast, hoping to avoid windless seas, and landed on the tip of Brazil. The country proved to be an agricultural treasure for Portugal, which profited from sugar plantations worked by enslaved Africans. Two hundred years later, gold and gemstones were discovered in Brazil, jump-starting the Portuguese economy again.

In 1520, Portuguese Ferdinand Magellan, although employed by Spain, sailed west with five ships and 270 men, broke for R&R in Rio, stopped in Patagonia, and continued through the straits that were later named for him (tip of South America); along the way he suffered through mutinies, scurvy, and dinners of sawdust and ship rats before touching land in Guam. Magellan was killed in battle in the Philippines, but one remaining ship continued west and arrived back in Europe, having circumnavigated the globe after 30 months at sea.

By 1560, Portugal's global empire had peaked. Tiny-but-filthy-rich Portugal claimed (though they didn't actually occupy) the entire coastline of Africa, Arabia, India, the Philippines, and south China—a continuous stretch from Lisbon to Macao—plus Brazil. The Treaty of Tordesillas (1494) with Spain had already divvied up the colonial world between the two nations, split at 45 degrees west longitude (bisecting South America—and explaining why Brazil speaks Portuguese and the rest of the continent speaks Spanish) and 135 degrees east longitude (bisecting the Philippines and Australia).

The Age of Discovery, 1400-1600

In 1560, you could sail from Lisbon to China without ever losing sight of land explored by Portugal. The riches of the world poured into the tiny nation—spices from India and Java (black pepper, cinnamon); ivory, diamonds, and enslaved people from Africa; sugarcane, gold, and diamonds from Brazil; and, from everywhere, knowledge of new plants, animals, and customs. How did tiny Portugal pull this off?

First, its people were motivated by greed, hoping to break the Arab and Venetian monopoly on Eastern luxury goods (the price of pepper was jacked up 1,000 percent by the time it reached European dinner tables). They pioneered—and profited from—the transatlantic slave trade, supplying enslaved Africans to Portuguese and Spanish colonies (all told Portugal ships are estimated to have transported over 4 million slaves to the New World).

They were also driven by a crusading Christian spirit, a love of science, and a spirit of adventure. An entire 15th-century generation was obsessed with finding the legendary kingdom of the fabulously wealthy Christian named "Prester John," supposedly located in either India or Africa. (The legend may be based on a historical figure from around 1120 who visited the pope in Rome as "patriarch of India.")

Portugal also had certain natural advantages. Its Atlantic location led to a strong maritime tradition. A unified nation-state (one of Europe's first) financed and coordinated expeditions. And a core of technology-savvy men used and developed their expansive knowledge of navigational devices, astronomy, maps, shipbuilding, and languages.

But all that wealth was wasted on Portugal's ruling class, who neglected to reinvest it in the future. Easy money ruined the traditional economy and stunted industry, hurting the poor. Over the next four centuries, one by one, Portugal's colonies were lost to other European nations or to local revolutions. Today, only the islands of the Azores and Madeiras remain from the once-global empire.

▲Belém Tower (Torre de Belém)

Perhaps the purest Manueline building in Portugal (built 1515-1520), this white tower protected Lisbon's harbor. Today it celebrates the voyages that made Lisbon powerful, with carved stone representing ropes, Manuel's coat of arms, armillary spheres, and shields with the cross of the Order of Christ, charged with spreading the faith in new territories. There's often a very long line to get into this tower, but there's nothing inside worth waiting very long to see.

Cost and Hours: €6, Tue-Sun 10:00-18:30, Oct-April until 17:30, closed Mon; from the monument it's a pretty, 15-minute waterfront walk, but be ready to detour around the big yacht marina; +351 213 620 034, www.torrebelem.pt.

Visiting the Tower: This was the last sight sailors saw as they left their homeland, and the first as they returned, loaded with gold, spices, and social diseases. When the tower was built, the river went nearly to the walls of the monastery, and the tower was midriver. Its interior is pretty bare, but the views of the bridge, river, and Cristo Rei statue are nice (though I prefer the lookout from the Monument to the Discoveries, which has a better view of the monastery).

The floatplane on the grassy lawn is a monument to the first flight across the South Atlantic (Portugal to Brazil) in 1922. The original plane (which beat Charles Lindbergh's *Spirit of Saint Louis* across the North Atlantic by five years) is in Belém's Maritime Museum.

MODERN LISBON AT PARQUE DAS NAÇÕES

Lisbon celebrated the 500th anniversary of Vasco da Gama's voyage to India by hosting Expo '98 here at Parque das Nações. The theme was "The Ocean and the Seas," emphasizing the global importance of healthy, clean waters. And today, the city has thoughtfully repurposed the fairgrounds into a residential area with parks and a shopping mall. To get out of the quaint, Pombal-esque old town and enjoy a peek at some modern architecture, ride the Metro to Oriente station. From here, you can stroll through an airy shopping mall, explore the sprawling site of the 1998 world's fair, and promenade with locals along the Rio Tejo riverfront park. It's worth a visit any day but makes most sense on Monday (when most museums in town are closed). It's also particularly vibrant when people are out early on summer evenings and weekends.

• *Your visit begins when you step off the train, inside...*

Oriente Train Station (Gare do Oriente)

Oriente means "facing east." This impressive hub ties together trains (to the Algarve and Évora), the Metro, and buses under a swooping concrete roof designed by the Spanish architect Santiago Calatrava.

• *Walk across the street to the Vasco da Gama Mall and look back at Oriente station: It looks like a futuristic sun-bleached fish skeleton. Look left and right and feel the urban energy. Learning from the mistakes of Sevilla's 1992 Expo, Lisbon made sure that its massive investment and construction for its Expo would plant the seeds for a thriving new neighborhood long after the party was over. Now step into the...*

Vasco da Gama Mall

The inviting, soaring glass facade of Lisbon's top shopping mall—originally the grand entrance to Expo '98—was also designed by Calatrava (daily 9:00-24:00). Inside, its design is reminiscent of a luxury cruise ship's main hall. Notice the water cascading down the glass roof—a clever and eye-pleasing way to keep things cool and avoid any greenhouse effect. From the mall's entrance, climb the stairs to a small outdoor terrace for a good view of the train station. Look up at the two skyscraping luxury condo buildings. With fine transportation connections and modern office space, this area holds lots of promise, both for residences and businesses. Microsoft set up its Portuguese headquarters in this area, cell phone giant Vodafone has one of the coolest buildings here, and the Portuguese national court occupies contemporary new buildings nearby.

Now stroll through the upper level of the mall to the opposite end, where (just past a big food court) you can step out to another outdoor terrace. From here you can look toward the river and survey Parque das Nações—the grounds for Expo '98. Straight ahead are the flags lining the Grand Esplanade (described next). The striped oval dome to the left, once the Atlantic Pavilion (Pavilhão Atlântico), is now an 18,000-seat concert hall. The oil refinery tower far to the right marks the west end of the park and is a remnant of the industrial wasteland that was here before the fair.

• *Exiting the mall at the far end from the train station, you'll be smack-dab in the middle of...*

▲▲Parque das Nações

From the Vasco da Gama Mall, you're at the top of the Grand Esplanade (Rossio dos Olivais), lined by 155 flags—one for each country represented at Expo '98. The flags are arranged in alphabetical order, so the first ones are South Africa (Africa dul Sul), Albania, and Germany (Alemanha). In the middle you'll find the US (Estados Unidos), Spain (Espanha), and Estonia side by side.

At the far end of the line of flags you'll reach a basin (on your right) that predates the fair. Back before World War II, this was a watery "parking lot" (just 1.5 yards deep) for seaplanes. Across the basin to your right, the blocky building that resembles an aircraft carrier with a spiky rooftop is the Lisbon Oceanarium (described next)—the big hit of the fair and still the park's major attraction. From behind that the cable car (€4 one-way, €6 round-trip, nothing special, daily 11:00-19:00) drifts east to the Vasco da Gama Tower, which marks that end of the park. Two miles away, built as part of the 1998 celebrations, is the Vasco da Gama Bridge. A delightful promenade (Caminho dos Pinheiros; "The Way of the Pine Trees") runs along the riverfront from the marina all the way to a park at the base of the Vasco da Gama Bridge.

Lisbon Oceanarium (Oceanário de Lisboa)

Europe's largest aquarium—housed in what looks like a drilling platform or a big, modern ship at sea—simulates four oceanic underwater and shoreline environments, from the Atlantic to the Pacific to the Indian to the Arctic. You'll circle around the upper level, seeing surface dwellers from each climate (such as otters, puffins, penguins, and other sea birds). Then you'll head downstairs and do another loop, this time seeing underwater creatures. The centerpiece—which you'll keep circling back to—is an enormous and mesmerizing central tank crammed full of fascinating fish big and small, including several sharks. Weekday-morning school groups are also happily on display.

Cost and Hours: €19, €10 for kids 4-12; €38.50 combo-ticket with 48-hour Gray Line hop-on, hop-off bus; daily 10:00-20:00, Nov-March until 19:00, last entry one hour before closing, +351 218 917 000, www.oceanario.pt.

Vasco da Gama Bridge (Ponte Vasco da Gama)

Europe's longest bridge (10.7 miles) was opened in 1998 to connect the Expo '98 grounds with the south side of the Rio Tejo, and to alleviate the traffic jams on Lisbon's only other bridge over the river, the 25th of April Bridge. The Vasco da Gama Bridge helped connect north and south Portugal, back when a freeway was a big deal in this late-to-develop European nation. Built low to the water, the bridge's towers and cables are meant to suggest the sails of a caravel ship.

EAST LISBON
▲National Tile Museum (Museu Nacional do Azulejo)

Filling the former Convento da Madre de Deus, the museum features piles of tiles, which, as you've probably noticed, are an art form in Portugal. The col-

lection occupies a stunning, tile-covered convent that received donations from buildings all over Portugal after the dissolution of religious orders in 1834. They've showcased the tiles as they would have originally appeared (note the diamond-shaped staircase tiles) and arranged the visit in chronological order. The presentation is low-tech to keep the focus on the beauty and diversity of this traditional handicraft. For aficionados, this is a handy one-stop survey. And the circa-1700 tile panorama of Lisbon (upstairs) is fascinating, letting you pick out landmarks that were toppled in the 1755 quake. Don't miss the cafeteria, covered in rescued tiles from a former smokehouse, appropriately painted with food-related themes.

Cost and Hours: €5; Tue-Sun 10:00-18:00, closed Mon; located about a mile east of Praça do Comércio—15 minutes on bus #794 from Praça do Comércio or bus #742 from near the Gulbenkian Museum (bus leaves around the corner from São Sebastião Metro station—along Rua Marquês de Fronteira), both buses stop right at museum entrance on Rua da Madre de Deus 4, +351 218 100 340, museudoazulejo.gov.pt.

SOUTH OF LISBON, ACROSS THE RIVER
Ferry Ride and Visit to Cacilhas

For an interesting and easy excursion to the small port town of Cacilhas (and a destination fish restaurant), catch the ferry from Lisbon for a 15-minute ride. The well-worn, graffiti-caked utility vessel is completely enclosed, serving thousands of daily commuters.

Getting There: The ferry leaves from the Cais do Sodré terminal (€1.25 each way, covered by public transit tickets/cards; at the ferry terminal, follow signs to *Cacilhas,* not *Montijo;* 4/hour, more during rush hours, less in evening, www.transtejo.pt). Plan on hitting or missing the rush-hour scene, depending on your taste. Upon arrival in Cacilhas, note when the next ferries return so you can plan your time smartly.

Visiting Cacilhas: The town's main street, **Rua Candido dos Reis,** is pedestrianized and charming, with lots of cute shops and eateries. The only "sight" in Cacilhas is the historic **Frigate *Don Fernando II and Gloria*** (Fragata *Dom Fernando II e Glória*), permanently moored at the dock. This was the last Portuguese ship to make the "Indian Run," which for three centuries connected Portugal with its colony in Goa. Launched in 1843 (and making its maiden voyage in 1845), in 33 years it sailed—defended by its 44 cannons—over 100,000 miles (the equivalent of five times around the world). It made its last trip in 1878, accidentally burned in 1963, and was rebuilt in 1997. Explore three decks for a taste of life on a 19th-century frigate. There's a guides' school nearby and you may find students standing by to give free tours as part of their training. The submarine drydocked adjacent was one of the Portugal navy's last subs (€4, Tue-Sun 10:00-18:00, Mon from 12:00, Oct-April daily until 17:00; buy booklet for English description, https://ccm.marinha.pt).

Eating in Cacilhas: **$$$ Restaurante Farol** is the best restaurant for eating fish—which is the reason most come to Cacilhas. The dining hall (no outside seating) is bright and airy with big view windows, an open kitchen, and an entire wall devoted to a blue-tile depiction of the spot and view in 1870 when this place opened (daily 12:00-23:00, 30 steps from the ferry terminal, on the right facing the river, +351 212 765 248).

Azulejos

During visits to neighboring Spain, King Manuel I not only acquired wives, but he also obtained
several thousand tiles to decorate
palaces throughout Portugal. Vibrant colors must have attracted
the king's attention, and some ex-
amples from his visits can still be
seen in the National Palace in Sintra. It wasn't long before Portuguese artists began producing
them for local clients, and the
tiles—called *azulejos* (ah-zoo-
LAY-zhoosh, from an Arab word
meaning "small polished stone")—
became synonymous with the
seafaring empire.

The biggest challenge for
early artisans was keeping colors
from running together during firing. A number of techniques
developed to solve this problem: *Alicatados* are mosaic pieces, cut after firing, to form intricate geometric patterns; *corda
seca* fills thick outlines of manganese oxide with different colors, like a children's coloring book; and *aresta* sculpts color
wells directly into the tile. The biggest breakthrough came
with the development of *majólica*, or *faiança*—the undecorat-
ed clay tile is baked first, then covered with an opaque glaze
that makes a canvas for the painted design, which is set by a
second firing.

Brazilians loved tilework, too, and after the return of the
Portuguese king to European shores, factories began producing tilework for the masses. But tilework began to fall out of
fashion by the early 20th century. Then Lisbon's 1959 Metro
system gave tile artists a new playground. While not originally
in the budget, artist Maria Keil could not bear to see the walls
vacant. Her original designs are still on display, and future artists continue to make the Metro an underground art museum.

Unfortunately, others have noticed the beauty (and prof-
itability) of historic tilework panels. Theft is common—often
for resale on the black market—and many of Lisbon's older
panels are at risk. In the past decade, local watch groups have
documented several hundred cases of missing panels and
helped recover several of them. And the law is changing to
help preserve Portugal's most visible art form; historic tiles
can now only be legally purchased via antique dealers. Please
don't purchase tilework at the Feira da Ladra flea market.

To go on your own *azulejo* scavenger hunt, check out
Endless Mile's tile guide to Lisbon that lists nearly 100 of the
city's best tile panels (www.endlessmile.com).

▲25th of April Bridge (Ponte 25 de Abril)

Imagine that before 1966, there was no way across the Rio Tejo except by ferry. This suspension bridge—1.5 miles long (3,280

feet between the towers—bears an uncanny resemblance to San Francisco's Golden Gate Bridge (it was built in 1966 by the same company that made its famous cousin—but notice the lower deck for train tracks). The foundations are sunk 260 feet below the surface into the riverbed, making it the world's deepest bridge. Originally named for the dictator Salazar, the bridge was renamed for the date of Portugal's 1974 revolution and liberation. For a generation, natives would show their political colors by choosing which name to use. While conservative Portuguese called it the "Salazar Bridge," liberals referred to it as the "25th of April Bridge" (just as Washington, DC's airport is still called "National" by some and "Reagan" by others).

Cristo Rei Statue (Christ the King)

A huge, 330-foot concrete statue of Christ (à la Rio de Janeiro, in the former Portuguese colony of Brazil) overlooks Lisbon from

across the Rio Tejo, stretching its arms wide to symbolically bless the city (or, as less reverent Portuguese say, "to dive into the river"). Lisbon's cardinal, inspired by a visit to Rio de Janeiro in 1936, wanted a replica built back home. Increased support came after an appeal was made to Our Lady of Fátima in 1940 to keep Portugal out of World War II. Portugal survived the war relatively unscathed, and funds were collected to build this statue in appreciation. After 10 years of construction, it opened to the public in 1959. It's now a sanctuary and pilgrimage site, and the chapel inside holds regular Sunday Mass.

The statue was designed to be seen from a distance, and there's little reason to go to the trouble of actually visiting it. If you do visit, an elevator will take you to the top for a panoramic view: From left to right, see Belém, the 25th of April Bridge, downtown Lisbon (Praça do Comércio and the green Alfama hilltop with the castle), and the long Vasco da Gama Bridge.

Cost and Hours: €5, daily 9:30-18:15, slightly later in summer, +351 212 751 000, www.cristorei.pt.

Getting There: To get to Cristo Rei, catch the ferry from downtown Lisbon to Cacilhas (described earlier in this section, under "Ferry Ride and Visit to Cacilhas"), then hop on the bus marked *101 Cristo Rei* (3/hour, exit ferry dock left into the maze of bus stops to find the #20 stop with the "101 Cristo Rei" schedule under the awning, 15-minute ride). Because of bridge tolls to enter Lisbon, taxis from the site are expensive. For drivers, the most efficient visit is a quick stop on your way to or from Évora or the Algarve.

WEST OF LISBON, ON THE COAST
Cascais

The seafront resort town of Cascais (kahsh-KAYSH), about 17 miles due west of Lisbon, provides a fun and quick escape from the big city of Lisbon. Before the rise of the Algarve, Cascais was the haunt of Portugal's rich and beautiful. Today it's an elegant and inviting escape from the city with pleasant beaches and a relaxing ambience.

Before the 20th century, aristocrats wanted to avoid the sun and exaggerate their lily-white skin—and a day at the beach made just no sense. But about 1900, the Portuguese queen Maria Pia (daughter of King Victor Emmanuel II of Italy) made Cascais her summer vacation getaway—and Portugal's high society followed. A train line made Cascais easily accessible from the city, and between the world wars, the area was developed as a kind of Portuguese answer to the French Riviera.

Getting There: Just hop the train at Lisbon's Cais do Sodré station (M: Cais do Sodré) and you're in Cascais in 40 minutes or less (3/hour, www.cp.pt).

Visiting Cascais: The Cascais station (the last stop on the Cais do Sodré line) faces the town center. From there, the main cobbled street, Rua Frederico Arouca, parallels the waterfront past shops and eateries to Largo Cidade Vitória, where you'll find a helpful TI kiosk (daily 9:00-18:00).

Cascais still has a fishing industry. Adjacent to the TI, you'll find the Serviços de Pescado, a wholesale fish market where most days at 17:00 visitors can witness the quick fish auction as local retailers snap up the day's catch. Just beyond is the main beach and a palm-lined promenade leading to an old fort. Deeper into town are several little museums; the Museu do Maris is best for the story of the town and its relationship with the sea (free, Tue-Sun 10:00-17:00, closed Mon, about 10 minutes from the center at Rua Júlio Pereira de Mello, www.cm-cascais.pt/museumar). Walk out for dramatic views at Boca do Inferno (a unique rock formation) to see what fishermen have to deal with.

Returning to Lisbon via Estoril: A paved seaside promenade leads from Cascais past several beaches to Estoril, its sister beach resort town (a half-hour stroll away). Of the several small sandy beaches, Praia da Conceição and Praia das Moitas conveniently have showers. If you have time and like seaside strolls, I'd recommend walking this strip and catching the train back to Lisbon from Estoril (all trains stop at both Estoril and Cascais).

Estoril is famous for its casino and many grand hotels. From the Lisbon-Cascais train you can look past the Estoril station and across the park at the modern casino. Ian Fleming hatched his first 007 story here in the early days of World War II, when Portugal was neutral and this area was a hotbed of spies. The Estoril casino where Fleming gambled must have been part of the inspiration for his first James Bond novel, *Casino Royale*. But Cascais rather than Estoril is clearly the most rewarding stop for today's traveler.

Shopping in Lisbon

Lisbon is a marvelous shopping city: creative, with a trendy vibe but also respectful of tradition—and it's affordable. My suggestions below focus on one-off shops that specialize in unique slices of Lisbon life. I've also included a few big malls for handy one-stop shopping.

WHAT TO BUY

The shops mentioned here are scattered around central Lisbon, but most are concentrated in the hip and artsy Chiado district.

Cork

Portugal is famous for its cork, a versatile material that can be put to hundreds of uses. Shops all over town show off practical and eye-pleasing items made of cork, from handbags to wallets to umbrellas. For fashionable, top-end products, head up to the flagship store of the internationally respected **Pelcor,** in the Príncipe Real shopping zone (Pátio do Tijolo 4, just off Rua Dom Pedro V, www.pelcor.pt). In the Bairro Alto, **Cork & Co** is a more affordable boutique with a wider array of products—including jewelry (closed Sun mornings, Rua das Salgadeiras 10, www.corkandcompany.pt).

Wine

If you're in the market to buy fine bottles of wine to enjoy in Portugal or to ship home, consider these two options. While touristy—and with somewhat inflated prices—both have helpful staff who can talk you through your options and arrange shipping. (They may suggest that you make your selection in the shop, then place your order on their website.) **Napoleão Wine Shop** has free samples of three unique Portuguese options: port, *vinho verde,* and *ginjinha* (daily, main branch at Rua Conceição 16 specializes in Portuguese wines, second branch across the street also has international booze; www.napoleao.eu). **Garrafeira Nacional** has a similar set-up in the Baixa (closed Sun, Rua da Conceição 20) and a user-friendly location open daily inside Mercado da Ribeira (www. garrafeiranacional.com).

Another place is **Wines of Portugal Tasting Room,** which sells regional favorites at affordable prices (many also available for tasting, Praça do Comércio, see details on page 37).

Azulejos (Colored Tiles)

Portugal's iconic colored tiles make vivid souvenirs—for use as trivets, wall hangings, or even (for the ambitious) a backsplash renovation project. It's easy to find affordable, basic, painted replicas of classic *azulejo* designs—many souvenir shops stock a small selection. For better-quality replica *azulejos,* try **Viúva Lamego** (closed Sat-Sun, Largo do Intendente 25), **Fábrica Sant'Anna** (closed Sun, in Chiado at Rua do Alecrim 95), or the more touristoriented **Loja dos Descobrimentos** (daily, below the cathedral at Rua dos Bacalhoeiros 12). If you're shopping for authentic antique tiles, try **d'Orey Azulejos** (closed Sun, in Chiado at Rua do Alecrim 68) or the cramped **Antiquário Solar** (a.k.a. Albuquerque e Sousa; closed Sat afternoon and all day Sun, in the Bairro Alto at Rua Dom Pedro V 68). Discontinued mid-20th-century industrial tiles (think solid colors but in bold relief) can be found at **Cortiço & Netos** (closed Sun, between Mouraria and the castle at Calçada de Santo André 66).

Conservas (Canned Fish)

Canned fish (collectively called *conservas*) is a Portuguese staple, are not the harsh, cured-in-salt sardines you might think of back home. This is quality fish in olive oil (sardines, cod, mackerel, and tuna are most common), often mixed with herbs, spices, or infused oils to impart extra flavor. Best of all, colorful packaging turns the cans into great souvenirs or gifts and makes window-shopping a delight. The best *conservas* place in town—near Mercado da Ribeira—is **Loja das Conservas,** with shelves upon shelves of attractively decorated cans from all over Portugal. This shop is operated by a local consortium, and prides itself on educating its customers

LISBON

To Pelcor
Cork & Co.
Napoleão Wine Shop
Garrafeira Nacional (2)
Wines of Portugal Tasting Room
To Viúva Lamego
Fábrica Sant'Anna
Loja dos Descobrimentos
d'Orey Azulejos
Antiquário Solar
Cortiço & Netos
Loja das Conservas

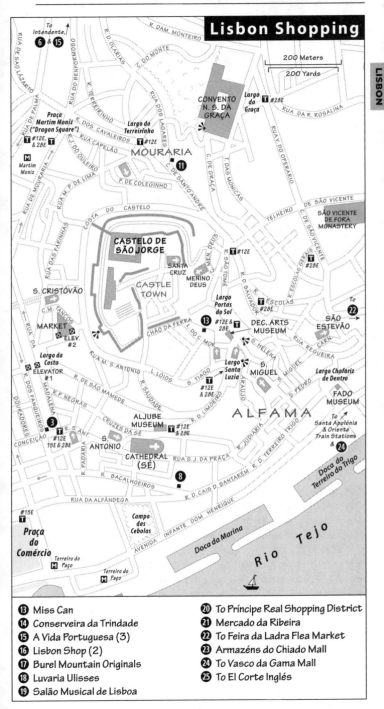

Lisbon Shopping

200 Meters
200 Yards

13 Miss Can
14 Conserveira da Trindade
15 A Vida Portuguesa (3)
16 Lisbon Shop (2)
17 Burel Mountain Originals
18 Luvaria Ulisses
19 Salão Musical de Lisboa

20 To Príncipe Real Shopping District
21 Mercado da Ribeira
22 To Feira da Ladra Flea Market
23 Armazéns do Chiado Mall
24 To Vasco da Gama Mall
25 To El Corte Inglés

(daily, Rua do Arsenal 130). In the upper part of the Alfama, just below the castle, **Miss Can** sells a small selection of their own production, with clever packaging and a little café where you can enjoy a light meal (see "Eating in Lisbon" later, daily, Largo do Contador Mor 19). And in Chiado, you'll find the upscale **Conserveira da Trindade,** with a carefully curated selection and the option to nibble right there (daily, Rua Nova da Trindade 11).

Other Quality Portuguese Souvenirs

A Vida Portuguesa is the best shop in town for a well-chosen selection of high-quality, artisanal Portuguese products—everything from stationery and toiletries to housewares and decorative objects to toys and jewelry (daily, Rua Anchieta 11, www.avidaportuguesa. com). They have two other locations: a bigger flagship store in the Intendente neighborhood (daily, Largo do Intendente 23), and a smaller location inside the Mercado do Ribeira.

If you're in a pinch for souvenirs, local TIs have a small but nicely stocked **"Lisbon Shop"** with some basic items emblazoned with Lisbon's trademarks—sardines, fado, or trolleys—as well as fado CDs, at prices typically better than elsewhere in the Baixa (daily, main branch in Praça do Comércio TI, smaller selection at the TI on Praça das Restauradores).

Woolens: The delightful **Burel Mountain Originals** boutique showcases fashionable items made from the heavy Portuguese wool called *burel*. This company took over an abandoned wool factory high in the mountains of northern Portugal and brought back skilled but out-of-work old-timers to revive a dormant industry. Today the factory churns out high-quality blankets, handbags, coats, shoes, and other products with a mix of traditional and contemporary style (daily, Rua Serpa Pinto 15B, www.burelfactory. com).

Leather Gloves: The Lisbon institution **Luvaria Ulisses** sells top-quality leather gloves *(luvas)* one pair at a time, with individual attention to help you find just the right style and fit. The shop is nestled into a tiny storefront just a few steps off Rossio. You squeeze into the shop, then the clerks squeeze your hands into the gloves: they'll nest your elbow on a dainty little pillow, squirt a puff of talcum powder into the glove, then massage your fingers in, one at a time (after a visit here, you'll better appreciate the expression "fits like a glove"). While popular with tourists from faraway lands (expect to wait at busy times), they're still cranking out quality gloves at decent prices (many pairs around €50-60, closed Sun, Rua do Carmo 87, www.luvariaulisses.com).

Musical Instruments: If you're captivated by fado and want to check out a Portuguese guitar, **Salão Musical de Lisboa** has a fine selection and a handy location, right on Largo do Carmo square (closed Sun, Rua da Oliveira ao Carmo 2, www.salaomusical.com).

WHERE TO SHOP
Consider a shopping spree in one of these areas.

Príncipe Real Shopping District
For cutting-edge fashion and design, and one of Lisbon's most appealing little green parks, head to the Príncipe Real Garden at the top of Chiado (about a five-minute walk, a speedy bus trip from the top of the Elevador da Glória funicular, or a stop on the #24E trolley route).

The anchor of this area is the **Embaixada** complex, across the street from the park. Young entrepreneurs have given a grand 19th-century Arabian-style townhouse a modern makeover and filled its two floors with goods from high-end local designers and vendors, attracting hipsters, well-dressed urbanites, and in-the-know tourists. You'll see fashion, home decor, kidswear, high-end tailors, art galleries, pop-up shops, and much more. Climb the grand old staircase, on scuffed tiles and under peeling plaster ceilings, to feel the artful "ramshackle chic" vibe. In the atrium, the Less café has affordable light meals and a gin bar; there's also a little garden café out back (daily 12:00-20:00, Praça do Príncipe Real 26).

Just a few doors down (walking with the park on your left), at the smaller but similarly chic **REAL "Slow Retail" Concept Store,** creative local vendors display their wares in a clean, cool, industrial-mod space. You'll see stacks of coffee-table books, creative housewares, summer dresses, burlap backpacks, colorful shoes and sandals, hipster toddler garb, and horn-rimmed sunglasses (Mon-Wed 10:30-20:00, Thu-Sat until 23:00, closed Sun, Praça do Príncipe Real 20).

A bit farther down are more fun shops, including **Corallo,** where Bettina and Niccolò make their own chocolates and roast their own coffee (closed Sun, Rua da Escola Politécnica 4), and the old-school **Príncipe Real Enxovais,** specializing in top-quality linens for the home (daily, Rua da Escola Politécnica 12). And in the opposite direction, a block up Rua Dom Pedro V back toward the heart of Chiado, is the **Pelcor** cork products flagship store (described earlier).

LISBON

This is also a great part of town to get a bite; for details, see the Chiado listings in "Eating in Lisbon," later.

Markets

Mercado da Ribeira (a.k.a. Time Out Market) is a renovated market hall offering Lisbon's best one-stop shopping for culinary souvenirs (it's described in detail on page 120). In addition to bottles of wine, chocolates, canned fish, and other edible goodies, it has an outpost of Lisbon's best souvenir shop, A Vida Portuguesa. And, of course, it's also great for a meal. Most restaurant stalls are open daily from 12:00 to 24:00. On Sunday mornings, a coin market jingles here. Note that the Loja das Conservas canned-fish shop is just down the street (described earlier).

On Tuesdays and Saturdays, the **Feira da Ladra flea market** attracts bargain hunters to Campo de Santa Clara in the Alfama (8:00-15:00, best in morning).

Shopping Malls and Department Stores

Lisbon has several malls and huge department stores (all open long hours daily). Most central is **Armazéns do Chiado,** with six modern floors—and handy elevators connecting the Baixa and Chiado (food court on the sixth floor, www.armazensdochiado.com). North of downtown, **Vasco da Gama Mall** fills the grand entryway to the Expo '98 site at the Oriente train/Metro station (described on page 85). And the Spanish megadepartment store, **El Corte Inglés,** has a huge branch at the top of Edward VII Park (near Gulbenkian Museum at Avenida António Augusto de Aguiar 31, M: São Sebastião).

Entertainment in Lisbon

NIGHTLIFE

The Baixa is quiet at night, with touristy al fresco restaurants and not much else. Head instead up to the Bairro Alto for fado halls, bars, and the Miradouro de São Pedro de Alcântara (view terrace), a pleasant place to hang out. Nearby Rua Diario de Noticias is lined with busy bars and fun crowds spilling onto the street.

Rua Nova do Carvalho (a.k.a. Pink Street)

This happening, crazy street is a short walk downhill from Chiado in the Cais do Sodré neighborhood (just behind Mercado da Ribeira). Rua Nova do Carvalho, otherwise known as "Pink Street," was once notorious as the sailors' red-light zone. Now the prostitutes are just painted onto the walls, and the made-over street is painted a bright pink. After the bars in other neighborhoods close, late-night revelers hike 10 minutes from Chiado down Rua do Alecrim to reach Pink Street. Surrounded by largely uninhabited Pombaline buildings, Pink Street's four bars are allowed to make noise—and they do—until very late into the night. Many of the nightspots here are rowdy, youthful dance halls with names like Tokyo, Musicbox, Viking, and Sabotage Rock Club, with a few striptease clubs mixed in. But the following places—lively earlier and accessible to a wider clientele—are my Pink Street picks.

Pensão Amor ("House of Love") is a velvety place for a cocktail. Wallpapered with sexy memories of the not-long-ago days when it was a brothel, it's a grungy tangle of corners to hang out in and enjoy a drink (or just stare at the graffiti), often against a backdrop of live jazz. It even has a sexy library if you feel like reading (no food, Rua Nova do Carvalho 38, also possible to enter from along the bridge at Rua do Alecrim 19, +351 213 143 399).

Sol e Pesca Bar, a nostalgic reminder of the sailor-and-fisherman heritage of this street, sells drinks and preserved food in tins. Just browse the shelves of classic tinned seafood—from pâté and sardines to caviar—and wash down your salty seafood tapas with a glass of wine amid the lures and nets (Rua Nova do Carvalho 44, +351 213 467 203).

Povo Lisboa is a trendy little bar serving delightful Portuguese tapas (from 18:00) and enlivening things with fado (Tue-Sun 20:30-23:00, closed Mon, no cover—just buy a drink, light food, Rua Nova do Carvalho 32, +351 213 473 403).

LX Factory

LX Factory is a typical riverside industrial zone gone hippie-chic. Passing through the factory gate (under the 25th of April Bridge), you'll find a youthful crowd sorting through a collection of restaurants, clubs, shops, and galleries. LX Factory

is lively each night and all day on weekends (www.lxfactory.com).

LISBON

Lisbon Nightlife

To Elevador do Lavra

R. DA GLORIA

R. ST. GLORIA

RUA TAIPAS

AVENIDA DA LIBERDADE

R. DA SÃO JOSE

CONDES

S. ANT.

COLISEU

ELEVADOR DA GLÓRIA

OBELISK

São Pedro de Alcântara Park

R. DOM PEDRO

RUA COELHO

TR. S. PEDRO

R. TEIXEIRA

R. S. ALCANTARA

R. MOUROS

C. DA GLORIA

Praça dos Restauradores

Restauradores

ABEP TICKET KIOSK

CALCADA WORKERS MEMORIAL

ROSSIO TRAIN STATION

REGEDOR

R. PORTAS S. ANTÃO

Largo de São Domingos

NAT'L THEATER

ROSSIO

RUA DA ROSA

TR. BOA HORA

IGREJA SÃO ROQUE

R. MISERICORDIA

MUSEU DE ARTE SACRA

Largo do Cadoval

Rossio (Praça Dom Pedro IV)

BAIXA

TR. AGUA FLOR

R. DO GREMIO

T. D. QUEIMADA

Largo Trindade Coelho

RUA C. DUQUE

R. DO DUQUE

RUA NOVA TRINDADE

R. DA CONDESA

R. DA OLIVEIRA

RUA 1 DEZEMBRO

RUA AUREA

ARCH

RUA LUZ SORIANO

BAIRRO ALTO

RUA GAVEAS

MUSIC SHOP

BAIRRO DO AVILLEZ

CONVENTO DO CARMO

ELEVADOR STA. JUSTA

R. DO OURO

R. DA ROSA

T. DOS FIEIS DE DEUS

NOTICIAS

R. BARROCA

❼

R. DO NORTE

TEATRO DA TRINDADE

R. DA TRINDADE

Largo do Carmo

TR. DO CARMO

R. DO CARMO

TR. MERCES

❺

❻

TV. ESPERA

❽

TR. TRIN.

CHIADO

R. DO CRUCIFIXO

To Miradouro de Santa Catarina

ELEVADOR DA BICA

R. CAL.

R. LORETO

T #28E

Praça Luís de Camões

RUA GARRETT

ARMAZÉNS DO CHIADO MALL

Largo Chiado

Baixa-Chiado

SERPA PINTO

A VIDA PORTUGUESA

Baixa-Chiado

R. D. CHAGAS

RUA H. SECA

T #28E

RUA S. FRAN.

R. ST. CAT.

T.G.

COUSSUL

BICA

❹

R. DA EMENDA

FLORES

RUA DO ALECRIM

RUA MARIA CARDOSO

RUA D. BRAGANÇA

RUA D. DE BRAGANÇA

R. ATAIDE

200 Meters

200 Yards

RUA NOVA DO CARVALHO

❷ ❶

"PINK STREET" (NIGHTLIFE)

RUA DO ARSENAL

MERCADO DA RIBEIRA

To Cais do Sodré Station

Cais do Sodré

Praça Duque de Terceira

Bars
❶ Pensão Amor & Povo Lisboa
❷ Sol e Pesca Bar

Wine
❸ Solar do Vinho do Porto
❹ By the Wine
❺ Lisbon Winery

Fado
❻ Restaurante Adega do Ribatejo
❼ O Faia
❽ Fado in Chiado

Serious Port Wine Tastings

Solar do Vinho do Porto, run by the Port Wine Institute, has per-haps the world's greatest selection of port—the famous fortified wine that takes its name from the city of Porto. If you're not headed to Porto, this is your best chance for serious exposure. The tasting room has been closed for renovation but should be reopened by the time you visit. The plush, air-conditioned, Old World living room is furnished with leather chairs (this is not a shorts-and-T-shirt kind of place). You can order from a selection of more than 150 dif-ferent ports (€2-22/glass). Fans of port describe it as "a liquid sym-phony playing on the palate." Read the instructive, easy menu for a do-it-yourself education. Start white and sweet (cheapest), taste your way through spicy and ruby, and finish mellow and tawny. A *colheita* (single harvest) is particularly good. Appetizers *(aperitivos)* are listed in the menu with small photographs. Table service can be slow and disinterested when it's busy; to be served without a long wait, go to the bar (Mon-Fri 11:00-24:00, closed Sat-Sun, across from top of Elevador da Glória funicular at Rua São Pedro de Alcântara 45).

Evening Stroll

In the summer, you'll find lots of people out strolling. Here are four good places to join them: Rua Augusta through the heart of the Baixa district; along the seaside promenade near Belém Tower; along the fine riverfront promenade at Parque das Nações; and the river walk at Ribeira das Naus (from the water at Praça do Comér-cio to Cais do Sodré).

FADO MUSIC

Fado is the ▲▲ folk music of Lisbon's back streets. Since the mid-1800s, it's been the Lisbon blues—mournfully beautiful and haunting ballads about lost sailors, broken hearts, and bittersweet romance. While generally sad, fado can also be jaunty—in a nos-talgic way—and captivating. An aging widow in a mourning shawl singing passionate fado can be as sexy as any performer.

While authentically traditional, most Lisbon fado bars cater to tourists these days. Don't expect to find a truly "local" scene. Even the seemingly homemade "fado tonight" *(fado esta noite)* signs are mostly for tourist shows. Still, if you choose well—and can find a convivial restaurant with relatively reasonable prices and fewer tour groups—it's a very memorable evening. (And be wary of your hotel's recommendations, which are often skewed by hefty kickbacks.)

The two main areas for fado in Lisbon are on either side of the Baixa: the Bairro Alto and the Alfama. Later, I've listed options in each neighborhood. To avoid disappointment, it's smart to reserve ahead.

Fado

Fado songs reflect Portugal's bittersweet relationship with the sea. Fado means "fate"—how fate deals with Portugal's adventurers...and the women they leave behind. These are songs of both sadness and hope, a bittersweet emotion called *saudade* (meaning yearning or nostalgia). The lyrics reflect the pining for a loved one across the water, hopes for a future reunion, remembrances of a rosy past or dreams of a better future, and the yearning for what might have been if fate had not intervened. (Fado can also be bright and happy when the song is about the virtues of cities such as Lisbon or Coimbra, or of the warmth of a typical *casa portuguesa*.)

The songs are often in a minor key. The singer *(fadista)* is accompanied by a 12-string Portuguese *guitarra* (with a round body like a mandolin) or other stringed instruments unique to Portugal. Many singers crescendo into the first word of the verse, like a moan emerging from deep inside. Though the songs are often sad, the singers rarely overact—they plant themselves firmly and sing stoically in the face of fate.

A verse from a typical fado song goes:

O waves of the salty sea,
where do you get your salt?
From the tears shed by the women in black
on the beaches of Portugal.

Ways to See Fado: Your basic choices are a polished restaurant with a professional-quality staged show; or—my preference—a more rustic place with *fado vadio*, a kind of open-mic fado evening when suspiciously talented "amateurs" line up at the door of neighborhood dives for their chance to warble. Waiters—hired more for their vocal skills than hospitality—sometimes take a turn entertaining the crowd.

Most people combine fado with a late dinner. The music typically begins between 20:00 and 21:00; arrive a bit earlier to be seated and order. Night owls can have a cheaper dinner elsewhere, then show up for fado when the first round of diners is paying their bills (around 22:30 or 23:00). Both elegant, high-end places and holes-in-the-wall generally let nondiners in late for the cost of an overpriced drink and/or a €10-15 cover charge.

Prices for Fado: Prices for a fado performance vary greatly, but assume you won't leave any fado experience without spending at least €30 per person—and more like €50-60 per person for the fancier restaurants. Many places have a cover charge, others just expect you to buy a meal, and some enforce a €25-30 per person minimum. Remember, as throughout Portugal, appetizers, bread, or cheese that appear on your table aren't free—if you don't want these appetizers, it's safest to push them aside.

Fado in the Bairro Alto

In the Bairro Alto, wander around Rua Diario de Noticias and neighboring streets.

Restaurante Adega do Ribatejo is a homey and crowded good budget option: Just pay for your meal (main courses around €15) and drinks with no cover or required minimum (daily 11:00-24:00, dinner from 19:00, Rua Diario de Noticias 23, +351 213 468 343). After 22:30, you're welcome to just buy a drink and enjoy the music.

O Faia is a top-end fado experience, in a classy dining room under heavy, graceful arches. It's pricey (plan on €60/person for dinner and drinks), but the food and the fado are both professional and top-quality. If you come after dinner (23:00) for just drinks and music, there's a €25 minimum. Filled with an older, well-dressed, international clientele, it's a memorable evening (open Mon-Sat for dinner at 20:00, fado begins at 21:30, closed Sun, Rua da Barroca 54, +351 213 426 742, www.ofaia.com).

Concert Alternative: Fado in Chiado, a sterile 50-minute performance in a small modern theater, is for tourists who don't want to stay out late or mess with a restaurant. Sitting with other tourists and without food or drink, you'll enjoy four musicians: a man and a woman singing, a guitarist, and a man on the Portuguese guitar, which gives fado its balalaika charm (€19,

daily at 19:00 except Sun, conveniently located at Rua da Misericordia 14, on second floor of in Cine Theatro Gymnasio, mobile +351 961 717 778, www.fadoinchiado.com).

Trendier Alternative: In the hip Rua Nova do Carvalho (a.k.a. Pink Street) nightlife zone, just downhill from the Bairro Alto and Chiado toward the river, **Povo Lisboa** has fado most nights (see listing earlier, under "Nightlife").

Fado in the Alfama

While often pretty lonely and dead after dark, the Alfama has several bars offering fado with their meals—just head uphill from the Fado Museum. Some bars are geared for tourists and tour groups, but others feel organic, spontaneous, and part of the neighborhood culture. While schedules at any particular place can be inconsistent, if you hike up Rua São Pedro de Alcântara to the Church of São Miguel, you'll hear the music wafting out from hole-in-the-wall eateries and be greeted by men hustling business for their fado restaurants. Generally, you simply pay for the meal and enjoy the music as included entertainment. If it's late and there's room, you can just buy a drink. For locations, see the "Alfama Restaurants" map, later.

A Baiuca, a tiny fun-loving restaurant, offers my favorite Alfama fado experience. A Baiuca—the name means a very rough tavern—packs people in and serves up spirited *fado vadio* (open mic for amateurs and waiters) with overpriced, basic food and lots of wine. As the English-speaking manager, Isabel, likes to say, "Fado needs wine." This intimate place has surround sound—as everyone seems to get into the music (€25 minimum—and be careful with the very pricey appetizers and bottles of wine that can push the bill much higher). If you come very late you can just buy a drink (music Thu-Mon 20:00-24:00, closed Tue-Wed, reservations smart, in the heart of the Alfama, just off Rua São Pedro up the hill from Fado Museum at Rua de São Miguel 20, +351 218 -867 284). When the door is closed, they're full, but you can peek at the action through the window around to the left.

Clube de Fado is much classier—one of the best places in town to hear quality fado. While expensive, there's not a bad seat in the house. Music plays nightly in this formal yet intimate setting. When busy, the musicians switch between two adjacent halls, giving waiters time to serve between sets, and diners get music about half the time (plan on €50/person for dinner with wine, plus €7.50 cover charge, meals from 20:00, dinner reservations required, music 21:30 until after midnight; after 23:00, pay just €10 cover plus cost of a drink; around corner from cathedral at Rua São João da Praça 94, +351 218 852 704, www.clube-de-fado.com).

Casa de Linhares, a block downhill from Clube de Fado, offers similar quality fado and an even nicer space, with dinner served under the stone vaults of a 16th-century palace (€15 cover for music, plan about €40/person for dinner, music nightly from 20:00, after 22:00 just cover plus drink purchase, Beco dos Armazéns Do Linho 2, +351 218 865 088, www.casadelinhares.com).

Concerts at the Fado Museum: At the base of the Alfama,

the Fado Museum hosts occasional live, free concerts that let you focus on the music (check schedule at www.museudofado.pt). Taking in a show here, then having a budget dinner elsewhere, lets you enjoy Alfama fado on the cheap.

BULLFIGHTS, SOCCER, CONCERTS, AND MOVIES

Tickets to bullfights, concerts, and other events are sold at the green **ABEP kiosk** at the southern end of Praça dos Restauradores (daily 9:00-20:00).

▲Portuguese Bullfight

If you always felt sorry for the bull, this is Touro's Revenge: In a Portuguese bullfight, the matador is brutalized along with the bull.

Lisbon hosts only about a dozen fights a year, but if you're in town for one, it's an unforgettable experience.

In Act I, the horseman *(cavaleiro)* skillfully plants four beribboned barbs in the bull's back while trying to avoid the leather-padded horns. The horses are the short, stocky Lusitano breed, with excellent balance. In Act II, a colorfully clad eight-man suicide squad (called *forcados*) enters the ring and lines up single file facing the bull. With testosterone sloshing everywhere, the leader taunts the bull—slapping his knees and yelling, *"touro!"*—then braces himself for a collision that can be heard all the way up in the cheap seats. As he hangs onto the bull's head, his buddies pile on, trying to wrestle the bull to a standstill. Finally, one guy hangs on to *o touro's* tail and "water-skis" behind him. (In Act III, the *ambulância* arrives.)

Unlike the Spanish *corrida de toros*, the bull is not killed in front of the crowd at the Portuguese *tourada*...but it is killed later. (Some brave bulls with only superficial wounds are spared to fight another day.) Spanish aficionados insist that Portuguese fights are actually crueler, since they humiliate the bull, rather than fight him as a fellow warrior. Animal-rights groups enliven the scene before each fight.

Fights are held at the **Campo Pequeno,** a spectacular, Moorish-domed brick structure that bears a resemblance to Madrid's bullring. The ring is small, so there are no bad seats. To sit nearly at ringside, try the cheapest *bancada* seats, on the generally half-empty and unmonitored main floor. Underneath the ring there's a shopping mall, and overhead there's a retractable roof for concerts. It hosts a variety of restaurants inside, including an Argentine steak restaurant. Maybe the beef served was in the ring earlier?

Cost and Hours: Tickets are always available at the door (€20-50); they're also sold at the ABEP kiosk on Praça dos Restauradores (10 percent surcharge). Fights are generally held from Easter through September, typically on Thursday evenings at 22:00; bullring is north of the Baixa in the Campo Pequeno district (M: Campo Pequeno); +351 217 932 143, www.campopequeno.com.

Important note: Half the fights are simply Spanish-type *corridas* without the killing. For the real slam-bam Portuguese-style fight, confirm that there will be *grupo de forcados* ("bull grabbers").

Soccer

Lisbon is home to two major league *futebol* teams, Benfica and Sporting CP, which means there are lots of games (1-2/week Aug-May, tickets €20 and up) and lots of team spirit. Benfica, with the red jerseys, plays at the 65,400-seat Stadium of Light, north of the city center (Estádio da Luz; M: Colégio Militar/Luz, www.slbenfica.pt). Sporting CP, with the green-and-white jerseys, plays at the 50,000-seat Estádio José Alvalade, which is also north of Lisbon's center (M: Campo Grande, www.sporting.pt). Tickets are generally available at the stadiums or at the ABEP kiosk on Praça dos Restauradores.

Concerts

The Gulbenkian Museum runs a classical concert season with about 180 events a year (www.gulbenkian.pt/musica). You can hear classical music by national and city orchestras at the cultural center in Belém (www.ccb.pt). Traditional Portuguese theater plays in the National Theater on Rossio, the fancy Teatro Nacional de São Carlos in Chiado, and in theaters along Rua das Portas de Santo Antão (the "eating lane"—described later, under "Eating in Lisbon") stretching north from Rossio. For popular music, these days you're more likely to find rock, jazz, Brazilian, and African music than traditional fado (which is more for tourists). The monthly *Agenda Cultural* provides the most up-to-date listing of world music, arts, and entertainment (free at TI, €0.50 at newsstands, online at www.agendalx.pt).

Movies

In Lisbon, unlike in Spain, films are shown in the original language with subtitles. (That's one reason the Portuguese speak better English than the Spanish.) Many of Lisbon's theaters are classy, complete with assigned seats, ushers, and intermissions. Check the newspaper or online to see what's playing. Modern options are in malls like Vasco da Gama (M: Oriente), El Corte Inglés (M: São

Sebastião), and at the Monumental complex in the ritzy Saldanha neighborhood (M: Saldanha).

Sleeping in Lisbon

Lisbon has a wide variety of accommodations. I've focused on a few categories: chic, international-style hotels offering a comfortable refuge at a high price; cheap, dingy, but affordable and safe old guesthouses (often up creaky old staircases in grimy buildings); boutique hotels offering a compromise between cost and comfort; and some famously classy hostels, which welcome travelers of all ages. For some travelers, short-term, Airbnb-type rentals can be a good alternative; search for places in my recommended hotel neighborhoods.

Lisbon has become increasingly popular, and rates have increased accordingly—especially on weekends (Thu-Sun), when many Brits and other Europeans fly in for brief urban vacations. Conventions can clog Lisbon at any time, and the busiest time is during the Festas de Lisboa (mainly the last three weeks of June) when parades, street parties, concerts, and fireworks draw crowds to the city.

I rank accommodations from **$** budget to **$$$$** splurge. To get the best deal, contact my family-run accommodations directly by phone or email. When you book direct, the owner avoids a commission and may be able to offer you a discount. Book well in advance for peak season or if your trip coincides with a major holiday or festival (see the appendix). For more information on reservations, short-term rentals, and more, see the "Sleeping" section in the Practicalities chapter.

THE BAIXA

Central as can be, the grid-planned, easy-to-navigate Baixa district bustles with shops, traffic, tourists, commuters, street musicians, pedestrian areas, and urban intensity. It's close to Rossio station, and the Aerobus to and from the airport cuts right through its middle. And it's handy to all of your sightseeing—wedged between the Alfama and the Bairro Alto/Chiado, with vintage trolleys zipping through every few minutes.

Upscale Hotels
$$$$ Internacional Design Hotel has 55 small, chic rooms centrally located at the southeast corner of Rossio. Each of its four floors has a different theme—pop, Zen, tribal, and urban. Having breakfast in their expansive restaurant overlooking Rossio is a fine way to start the day (air-con, elevator, underground pay parking nearby, Rua da Betesga 3, +351 213 240 990, www.idesignhotel. com, book@idesignhotel.com).

LISBON

Lisbon Center Hotels

To Praça Marquês de Pombal & Gulbenkian Museum

OBELISK

Praça dos Restauradores

Restaura-dores Ⓜ

ABEP TICKET KIOSK

Restaura-dores

São Pedro de Alcântara Park

ELEVADOR DA GLÓRIA

❽

❷

ROSSIO TRAIN STATION

Largo do Cadoval

IGREJA SÃO ROQUE

MUSEU DE ARTE SACRA

Largo Trindade Coelho

R. C. DUQUE

⓱ R. DO DUQUE ⓲

R. CONDESA

R. DA OLIVEIRA

⓮

CONVENTO DO CARMO

BAIRRO ALTO

⓲

TEATRO DA TRINDADE

⓭

R. DA TRINDADE

Largo do Carmo

⓰

R. DO CARMO

CHIADO

RUA GARRETT

ELEVADOR DA BICA

⓳

#28E

Praça Camões

#28E

Baixa-Chiado Ⓜ

Largo Barão Quintela

SÃO CARLOS THEATER (OPERA)

R. CAPELO

⓯

BICA

To Belém & ⓴

100 Meters
100 Yards

❶ Internacional Design Hotel
❷ Hotel Avenida Palace
❸ My Story Hotel Rossio
❹ My Story Hotel Tejo
❺ My Story Hotel Ouro
❻ Pensão Praça da Figueira
❼ Pensão Residencial Gerês

LISBON

8 Lisbon Destination Hostel
9 Home Lisbon Hostel
10 Living Lounge Hostel
11 Lisbon Lounge Hostel
12 Casa Balthazar
13 Lisboa Carmo Hotel
14 Lisboa Pessoa Hotel

15 Casa do Barão
16 Feeling Chiado 15
17 Zuza Guest House & Zuzabed & Breakfast
18 Zuzabed Lisbon Suites
19 Chiado 44
20 To Hotel As Janelas Verdes
21 Laundry (2)

$$$$ Hotel Avenida Palace, the most characteristic five-star splurge in town, was built with Rossio station in 1892 to greet big-shot travelers. Back then, trains were new, and Rossio was the only station in town. The lounges are sumptuous, dripping with chandeliers, and the 82 rooms—while a bit faded—still mix elegance with modern comforts (air-con, elevator, free parking, hotel's sign is on Praça dos Restauradores but entrance is at Rua 1 de Dezembro 123—down a small alleyway next to Starbucks, +351 213 218 100, www.hotelavenidapalace.pt, reservas@hotelavenidapalace.pt).

Boutique Chain Hotel: The **$$$ My Story** chain offers stylish, efficient rooms in the most central part of Lisbon. The combination of smart design plus friendly service makes these branches a reliable choice in the Baixa. All have air-conditioning and elevators and share a website (www.mystoryhotels.com). **My Story Hotel Rossio** rents 46 well-equipped, rooms in a couldn't-be-better location, tucked behind a strip of cafés facing bustling Rossio (Praça Dom Pedro IV 59, +351 213 400 380, rossio@mystoryhotels.com). **My Story Hotel Tejo** occupies two entire buildings with 135 rooms on the site of an old well. Street-side rooms on upper floors have a castle view (Rua Condes de Monsanto 2, +351 218 866 162, tejo@mystoryhotels.com). **My Story Hotel Ouro** has 51 rooms decorated in gold tones. Outside-facing rooms have great views, with double-paned windows over the busy streets below, but for maximum quiet, ask for an inside or upper-floor room (Rua Áurea 100, +351 213 400 340, ouro@mystoryhotels.com).

Affordable Dives

Basically a notch up from a hostel, these listings are worth considering if you're on a tight budget and want a handy Baixa location. Keep in mind that you get what you pay for—these are the best I've found in this price bracket.

$ Pensão Praça da Figueira is a backpacker place on a quiet back street with youth-hostel prices, a kitchen on every floor, a slick modern lobby overlooking Praça da Figueira, and 34 basic but colorfully updated rooms—some with views on the square (cheaper rooms have shared bath but no air-con, 2 flights up with no elevator, entrance is at Travessa Nova de São Domingos 9, +351 213 426 757, www.pensaopracadafigueira.com, reservas@ppf.com).

$ Residencial Florescente rents 67 straightforward rooms on the thriving, traffic-free "eating lane," a block off Praça dos Restauradores (air-con, elevator, Rua das Portas de Santo Antão 99—for location see "Lisbon's Avenida da Liberdade" map, later, +351 213 426 609, www.residencialflorescente.com, geral@residencialflorescente.com).

$ Pensão Residencial Gerês is a throwback, renting 20 well-worn, no-frills rooms with double-paned windows. The sweet

Nogueira family speaks some English (RS%, cheaper rooms with private bathroom down the hall, no breakfast, uphill a block off northeast corner of Rossio, Calçada do Garcia 6, +351 215 958 368, no website but book at www.booking.com, infogereslx@gmail.com).

Boutique Hostels in the Baixa

Among hostel aficionados, Lisbon is famous for having the best hostels anywhere. They welcome travelers of any age, come with an artistic flair, and, besides the usual dorm beds, have plenty of double rooms (except Home Lisbon Hostel). These come with extras like bike rental, movie nights, and cheap or "free" (tip-based) city tours and excursions out of town.

¢ **Lisbon Destination Hostel** feels designed for backpackers—young and old—who appreciate style, peace, and quiet. Located upstairs in the Rossio train station (literally next to the platforms), it provides a wonderful value and experience. The astroturfed lounge—with beanbag chairs and hammocks—sprawls beneath an Industrial Age glass canopy (many private rooms available, movie night in lounge, Largo do Duque de Cadaval 17, +351 213 466 457, www.destinationhostels.com, lisbon@destinationhostels.com).

¢ **Home Lisbon Hostel** is a little more rough and homey, with a loose camaraderie and friendly management. The hostel is dominated by its classic old wooden bar—an inviting place to socialize (7 private rooms—the rest are dorms, on the second floor at Rua de São Nicolau 13, near corner of Rua dos Fanqueiros, M: Baixa-Chiado, +351 218 885 312, www.homelisbonhostel.com, info@homelisbonhostel.com).

¢ **Living Lounge Hostel** is clean, modern, and centrally located near the Baixa-Chiado Metro stop. Each room is uniquely decorated (private rooms including singles, some rooms with air-con, Rua Crucifixo 116, second floor, +351 213 461 078, www.livingloungehostel.com, info@livingloungehostel.com).

¢ **Lisbon Lounge Hostel,** run by the same folks as the Living Lounge Hostel (above), is roughly midway between Praça da Figueira and Praça do Comércio (private rooms but no singles, Rua de São Nicolau 41, +351 213 462 061, www.lisbonloungehostel.com, info@lisbonloungehostel.com).

CHIADO

The Chiado district feels like Lisbon's uptown. For many, it's the best of all worlds: It's handy to the Baixa and Rossio area (just a few steps downhill), and to the artfully seedy Bairro Alto fado zone (just a few steps uphill), but it feels less touristy and congested than either. It's also a prime location for Lisbon's up-and-coming foodie restaurants and hipster shopping scene, making this a fun place simply to wander, graze, and window-shop. If I were buying an apartment in Lisbon, I'd look in Chiado. This area specializes in fresher, small, conscientiously-run boutique hotels—often upstairs in big buildings without elevators (expect lots of stairs).

$$$$ Casa Balthazar is an enticing splurge—an oasis-like private compound of stately old townhouses tucked amid characteristic, restaurant-lined stepped lanes just above Rossio, on the way up into the heart of Chiado. Classy and modern but still homey, each of its 17 rooms is different—some with views, terraces, and/or private whirlpool baths. There's an inviting little swimming pool, and breakfast is served in your room (air-con, Rua do Duque 26, mobile +351 917 085 568, www.casabalthazarlisbon.com, reservas@casabalthazarlisbon.com).

$$$$ Lisboa Carmo Hotel is bigger and has less personality than the others listed here, but it's in an appealing location: a few steps from charming Largo do Carmo. It has 48 sleek, straightforward, business-class rooms, not much in the way of public spaces, and the only elevator among my Chiado listings (air-con, elevator, Rua da Oliveira ao Carmo 1A, +351 213 264 710, carmo.luxhotels.pt, lisboa.carmo@luxhotels.pt). Their newer sister property, **$$$$ Lisboa Pessoa Hotel,** has similar rooms and a swimming pool just up the street in a neatly tiled building.

$$$ Casa do Barão is a delightful little refuge on a tame sidestreet just a block below the bustling Praça Luís de Camões in the heart of Chiado. Its 14 tidy, well-appointed, modern rooms share several fine common spaces, including a cozy library, winter-garden breakfast room, gravel patio, and tiny swimming pool. Complimentary coffee, tea, and snacks are available all day. At the lower end of this price range, it's a terrific value and a comfortable home base in Lisbon. As it's not staffed 24 hours a day, confirm your arrival details (air-con, Rua da Emenda 84, mobile +351 967 944 143, www.casadobarao.com, casasdobarao@gmail.com).

$$$ Feeling Chiado 15 is a fourth-floor walk-up with eight rooms high above the most appealing little leafy square, Largo do Carmo. Four of the rooms—at the cheaper end of this price range—look down over a residential patio; the pricier, "deluxe" rooms have views over Lisbon's rooftops and castle (most rooms have air-con, Largo do Carmo 15, +351 213 470 845, www.feelingchiado.com, feelingchiado@gmail.com).

Zuza, run by entrepreneurial Luis Zuzarte, has rooms in three different buildings around Chiado. The main branch, **$ Zuza Guest House,** has eight basic but neatly outfitted rooms with shared bathrooms in a creaky old building (no air-con, Rua do Duque 41). A few doors down, **$$ Zuzabed & Breakfast** has four rooms with bathrooms and castle views (air-con, Calçada do Duque 29). And a short walk away, up in the Bairro Alto, **$$$ Zuzabed Lisbon Suites** has seven classy rooms with vintage furnishings (Rua das

Gáveas 81). Let them know when you'll arrive: Morning check-in is likely at the Rua do Duque location; otherwise it'll be at the location you're sleeping at (contact for all: mobile +351 934 445 500, www.zuzabed.com, zuzabed@zuzabed.com).

$$ Chiado 44 is a simple place in a great location, just above Praça Luís de Camões. Its 11 small, basic, but comfortable rooms fill a historic building—expect plenty of stairs (air-con, Rua Horta Seca 44, mobile +351 918 352 901, www.chiado44.pt, info@chiado44.pt, Fabian).

ALONG AVENIDA DA LIBERDADE

Avenida da Liberdade is an upscale neighborhood facing a broad, tree-lined, very European-feeling boulevard. Most of my listings are a block or so off the main street. While it's a residential area, there are also lots of hotels—it's where many of Lisbon's tourists go to sleep. For this reason, it's a bit less characteristically "Lisbon" than some other neighborhoods...but for the sake of a quiet night's sleep, some consider that a good thing. These listings are a 10-minute walk or short Metro ride from the center. Most are near the Avenida Metro stop; Lisbon Dreams is closer to the Rato station.

High-End Chain Hotels

The **Hoteis Heritage Lisboa** chain has several branches, most near Avenida da Liberdade. These hotels distinguish themselves with classy public spaces and rooms, professional staff, and top-notch amenities (air-con, elevator, pay parking); guests are entitled to sightseeing deals—ask for details. Each hotel has its own style and personality, and all offer free port wine after 18:00 (www.heritage.pt).

$$$$ Hotel Britania maintains its 1940s Art Deco charm throughout its 33 spacious rooms, offering a clean and professional haven on a workaday street one block off Avenida da Liberdade. Three top-floor rooms are decorated in a luxurious Mod Deco style (Rua Rodrigues Sampaio 17, +351 213 155 016, britania.hotel@heritage.pt).

$$$$ Heritage Avenida Liberdade is the most contemporary, the only one actually on the leafy boulevard, and the closest to the center (a 5-minute walk from Rossio). Its stylish lobby/breakfast room is inviting, and the 42 rooms feel upscale-urban (Avenida da Liberdade 28, +351 213 404 040, avliberdade@heritage.pt).

$$$ Hotel Lisboa Plaza—a large, plush gem—mixes traditional style with bright-pastel classiness. Its 112 rooms are on a quiet street off busy Avenida da Liberdade, a block from the Avenida Metro station (Travessa do Salitre 7, +351 213 218 218, plaza@heritage.pt).

West of the Center: Another Hoteis Heritage branch is farther out, toward Belém. **$$$$ Hotel As Janelas Verdes** is next door to

Lisbon's Avenida da Liberdade

Accommodations
1. Hotel Avenida Palace
2. Residencial Florescente
3. Hotel Britania
4. Heritage Avenida Liberdade
5. Hotel Lisboa Plaza
6. Hotel Alegria
7. Lisbon Dreams Guest House

Eateries
8. Pinóquio Restaurante
9. Bonjardim Restaurantes
10. Casa do Alentejo Restaurante & Bar
11. Restaurante Solar dos Presuntos
12. Cantinho São José
13. Cervejaria Ribadouro
14. Restaurante A Gina
15. Quermesse Restaurante
16. Esplanada do Príncipe Real
17. A Cevicheria
18. Pavilhão Chines

the Museum of Ancient Art, filling an 18th-century mansion with 29 cushy rooms and comfortably elegant public spaces. The third-floor library overlooks the river (Rua das Janeles Verdes 7, bus #714 stops nearby, +351 213 968 143, janelas.verdes@heritage.pt).

Other Avenida Liberdade Hotels

$$$ Hotel Alegria faces a quiet, inviting park in a peaceful neighborhood 200 yards from the Avenida Metro station. Its bright, inviting public spaces and 30 comfortable, well-appointed rooms have hardwood floors varnished like a ship's deck (breakfast extra, air-con, elevator, Praça da Alegria 12, +351 213 220 670, www. hotelalegria.pt, info@hotelalegria.pt).

$ **Lisbon Dreams Guest House** has 18 fresh, relaxing, Ikea-style rooms, occupying three apartments and sharing seven bathrooms (shared kitchen and terraces; M: Marquês de Pombal, then take Rua Alexandre Herculano uphill and turn left on Rua Rodrigo da Fonesca, or M: Rato, take Rua Alexandre Herculano downhill, then right to reach Rua Rodrigo da Fonesca 29, +351 213 872 393, www.lisbondreams.com, reservations@lisbondreams.com).

Eating in Lisbon

Each district of the city comes with fun and characteristic restaurants. (Good eateries in Belém are described on page 72.) Ideally, have one dinner with a fado performance—several good options for music with your meal are listed in this section, with more fado options described earlier, under "Entertainment in Lisbon." Note that some smaller, family-run places take a few weeks off in the late summer or early fall—don't be surprised to find a handwritten *fechado para férias* (closed for vacation) sign taped to the window. For a great fish meal, combine a quick and fun ferry ride across the river to Cacilhas to dine at the grand **Restaurante Farol,** described on page 88.

Snack Bars: Quick, light meals are readily found in Lisbon's characteristic snack bars. On just about any street, you can belly up to a bar, observe, and order what looks good for a tasty, memorable, and inexpensive meal. You'll see lots of *pastel de bacalhau,* Lisbon's ubiquitous and delicious cod cake. Other good standbys are a *tosta* (panini filled with tuna or ham and cheese), a *prego* (steak sandwich) and a *bifana* (pork sandwich), each made with a secret sauce to give them character.

Food Tours in Lisbon: To simultaneously eat good food, learn about Portuguese cuisine, and meet a knowledgeable local guide, consider taking one of the food tours (described on page 24). These tours are informative, tasty, and a good value—filling you in while filling you up.

I rank eateries from $ budget to $$$$ splurge. For more advice on eating in Portugal, including ordering, tipping, and Portuguese cuisine and beverages, see the "Eating" section of the Practicalities chapter.

THE BAIXA AND NEARBY
On or near Rossio

The area around Rossio, with plenty of practical, inexpensive eateries, caters to busy locals commuting in and out by train. For locations, see the "Lisbon Center Restaurants" map on page 118.

$$$ Bastardo Restaurante—upstairs in the recommended Internacional Design Hotel—is a simple, solid, no-stress option for Portuguese cuisine with a modern twist overlooking the square. In a fun-loving way, they've bastardized traditional dishes. They also offer a classic Portuguese €15 lunch special. The space is fresh, bright, and accessible, like the menu. It can be smart to reserve (vegan options, daily 12:30-22:30, Rua da Betesga 3, facing Rossio, +351 213 240 993, http://restaurantebastardo.com).

$$ Confeitaria Nacional has been proudly satisfying sweet tooths for 180 years, and was once the favorite of Portuguese royalty. Stop in for a tasty pastry downstairs. Or, for a peaceful and inexpensive lunch, go upstairs, where you'll choose between a cheaper meal in the cafeteria or pay a little extra for service and Old World sophistication in the elegant dining room (Mon-Sat 8:00-20:00, pastry counter open Sun but upstairs may be closed, Praça da Figueira 18, +351 213 424 470).

$$ Café Nicola, founded in the 18th century as one of first coffee shops in town, was long a hangout of cultural elites. You'll find an Art Deco interior, formal waiters, and lots of locals eating its Nicola pepper steak. It's a sprawling, venerable café scene with classy seating inside and on the wide sidewalk facing Rossio's square (daily 8:00-24:00, Praça Dom Pedro IV 24, +351 213 460 579).

$ Casa Brasileira offers a characteristic budget snack or meal in a classic local scene. Fast lunch deals are served only at the bar (see blackboard at back for daily special); good, basic meals are served outside on sidewalk tables. Their *pastel de nata* (custard tart), made downstairs and in a second thriving kitchen next door, is as tasty as those that people line up for in Belém (daily 7:00-24:00, 100 yards from Rossio at Rua Augusta 265, +351 213 459 713).

$ Restaurante Beira-Gare is my choice for a quick, cheap meal immediately across the street from Rossio station. A classic greasy-spoon diner, it dishes out cod and vegetables prepared faster than a Big Mac and served with more energy than a soccer team. The house specialty is a pork sandwich *(bifana)*. Consider their soup-and-sandwich special; stand at the bar, grab a table, or sit outside for the pedestrian commotion (Mon-Sat 6:00-24:00, closed Sun, Rua 1 de Dezembro, +351 213 420 405). This is a great place for a quick cod cake *(pastel da bacalao)* at the bar.

Dive Bar with a View: Established in 1840 and run by Calheiros and Carmo, **$ A Tendinha do Rossio** is a classic *ginjinha* bar that also sells soups, sandwiches, and fishy snacks. While it's pretty dumpy, it's notable because it offers the only cheap tables on Rossio. Prices are dirt-cheap and the same whether you sit with the drunks at the bar, grab a tiny table inside, or serve yourself and sit outside overlooking Rossio (Mon-Sat 7:00-21:00, closed Sun, Praça Dom Pedro IV 6, +351 213 468 156).

Rua 1 de Dezembro: This street, which is active during the workday and dead after hours, is lined with cheap restaurants that make self-service speed a priority for busy office workers who eat here. Walk the street from Rossio station to the Elevador de Santa Justa to determine the prevailing menu of the day. Among your options is the handy self-service cafeteria at #97, **$$ Leão d'Ouro,** with an affordable lunch or dinner buffet featuring Brazilian grilled meats. It also has a fancy and more expensive sit-down restaurant next door (both daily 12:00-23:00).

There are two **grocery stores** on this street, both open long hours daily: the straightforward **Pingo Doce supermarket** (at #73, with very cheap 9-stool cafeteria), and the organic/health-food alternative across the street, **Celeiro,** which also has a self-service vegetarian lunch joint (called Tasquinha do Celeiro, at #53, Mon-Fri 8:00-18:00, closed Sat-Sun).

Lisbon's "Eating Lane" and Nearby

Just north of Rossio, Rua das Portas de Santo Antão is Lisbon's "eating lane"—a galaxy of eateries, many specializing in seafood (off the northeast corner of Rossio). While the waiters are pushy and it's all very touristy, the lane—lively with happy eaters—is enjoyable to browse. This is a fine spot to down a beer, snack on some snails, and watch people go by. For locations, see the "Lisbon's Avenida da Liberdade" map, on page 114.

$$$ Pinóquio Restaurante, a venerable seafood beer hall famous for its clams (€22 splittable portion), has a good local energy. You'll dine with a smart crowd at white-tableclothed tables yet with no pretense—the focus is on simple quality (daily 12:00-24:00, big portions, dine inside or outside facing the busy square, Praça dos Restauradores 79, +351 213 465 106).

$$ Bonjardim, a family-friendly diner on a small side street, is known for its tasty rotisserie chicken (pour on some spicy *piri-piri* sauce). Try their wonderful takes on *pastéis de bacalhau* (codfish fritters) or *esparregado* (spinach purée with garlic and olive oil), both Portuguese classics (daily 12:00-23:00, Travessa do Santo Antão 7 or 10, both branches run by same owner, one branch closes for a day off each week but the other takes up the slack, +351 213 427 424).

$$$ Casa do Alentejo Restaurante specializes in Alentejo

LISBON

Lisbon Center Restaurants

S. ANT.

OBELISK

Praça dos Restauradores

R. DOM PEDRO V

RUA TAIPAS

São Pedro de Alcântara Park

To Praça Marquês de Pombal & Gulbenkian Mus

R. COELHO

T. S. PEDRO

C. DA GLÓRIA

R. S. P. ALCÂNTARA

R. TEIXEIRA

Restaura-dores Ⓜ

R. REGEDOR

ℹ

ABEP TICKET KIOSK

Restaura-dores Ⓜ

K. MOUROS

RUA DA ROSA

K. S. B. VEN.

TK. BOA HORA

ELEVADOR DA GLÓRIA

ROSSIO TRAIN STATION

IGREJA SÃO ROQUE

TR. AGUA FLOR

MUSEU DE ARTE SACRA

See Avenida da Liberdade detail map

Ⓐ 7

Largo do Cadoval

RUA DA ATALAIA

R. DO GREMIO

R. MISERICORDIA

Largo Trindade Coelho

R. C. DUQUE

Ⓐ 18 R. DO DUQUE

Ⓐ 19

TR. QUEIMADA

R. CONDESA

Ⓐ 29

R. DA OLIVIERA

BAIRRO ALTO

RUA DA ROSA

NOTICIAS

R. DO NORTE

RUA GAVEAS

Ⓐ 28 Ⓐ 15

Ⓐ 24

RUA NOVA TRINDADE

CONVENTO DO CARMO

TR. DOS FIEIS DE DEUS

TEATRO DA TRINDADE

R. DA TRINDADE

Largo do Carmo

Ⓐ 30

R. BARROCA

R. ESPERA

Ⓐ 14

T. MERCES

TR. DO CARMO

Ⓐ 31

CHIADO

To Ⓐ 32

Ⓐ 22

R. CAL. R. LORETO

Ⓣ #28E

Praça Camões

RUA GARRETT

ELEVADOR DA BICA

Ⓣ #28E

Ⓜ Baixa-Chiado

R. H. SECA

R. SERPA PINTO

R. DA EMENDA

R. D. CHAGAS

Ⓝ

Largo Barão Quintela

Ⓐ 16

Ⓐ 25

Ⓐ 23

R. ST. CAT.

T. G. COUSSUL

RUA DO ALECRIM

RUA A. MARIA CARDOSO

RUA D. DE BRAGANÇA

R. CAPELO

BICA

Ⓐ 17

RUA FLORES

SÃO CARLOS THEATER (OPERA)

Ⓐ 20

BIBLIOTECA PUBLICA

R. ATAIDE

To Belém ←

100 Meters

100 Yards

Ⓐ 26

RUA S. PAULO

Ⓐ 27

RUA VITOR CÓRDON

Ⓐ 13

Baixa & Nearby

1. Bastardo Restaurante
2. Confeitaria Nacional
3. Café Nicola
4. Casa Brasileira
5. Restaurante Beira-Gare
6. A Tendinha do Rossio
7. Leão d'Ouro Rest./Buffet
8. Pingo Doce Supermarket
9. Celeiro Supermarket/Café
10. To Tentações de Goa
11. To Cervejaria Ramiro
12. Nova Pombalina

Chiado

13. Restaurante Vicente
14. Carmo Restaurante & Bar
15. Cervejaria da Trindade
16. Palácio Chiado
17. By the Wine
18. Café Buenos Aires & Solar do Duque
19. El Rei D'Frango
20. Café no Chiado
21. Armazéns do Chiado Mall
22. Manteigaria
23. Belcanto
24. Bairro do Avillez Taberna & Páteo
25. Café Lisboa
26. Cantinho do Avillez
27. Pizzaria Lisboa
28. Pitaria

Barrio Alto

29. Restaurante Bota Alta
30. A Primavera do Jerónimo
31. Lisbon Winery
32. To Mercado de Campo de Ourique
33. Martinho da Arcada Café Bar
34. Wines of Portugal Tasting Room

Lisbon's Gourmet Food-Circus Markets

The big news on Lisbon's eating scene is the transformation of traditional farmers markets into gourmet food circuses. These combine the stalls of traditional food-market vendors (selling produce, meat, fish, spices, etc.) with a food court filled with eateries run by locally respected chefs. If you love food—or even if you don't—these are fun to explore.

Mercado da Ribeira (a.k.a. Time Out Market)

Located at Cais do Sodré (between Chiado and the river), this is two markets in one: The bois-
terous and venerable Ribeira market survives in one half of the Industrial Age, iron-and-glass market hall, while the other half has become a trendy food court curated by *Time Out* magazine, which has invited a few dozen quality restaurants to open outposts here. Eating here at long, noisy picnic tables is far from romantic,

but the quality and prices are great. The produce and fish market is open from 7:00 to 13:00 (closed Sun and no fish Mon), while the restaurants are open daily from 12:00 to 24:00. This place is no secret—to avoid a mob scene at dinnertime, arrive before 19:00.

Getting There: The Mercado da Ribeira (like many locals, I resist calling this venerable market by its new "Time Out" name) is across the street from the Cais do Sodré train station. It's conveniently served by the Metro (Cais do Sodré stop) and tram #15E (on the way to/from Belém), and it's about a 10-minute walk from Praça do Comércio. If you're here for dinner, note that the crazy Pink Street—lined with clubs and bars—is just two blocks inland and lively late (described in "Entertainment in Lisbon," earlier). The entire neighborhood around the market is emerging as a lively and trendy food and bar scene.

Eating at Mercado da Ribeira: Entering the market from the main entrance (facing Cais do Sodré), the workaday market stalls are on your right, while the foodie festival is on your left. In

cuisine and fills an old, second-floor dining hall. The Moorish-looking building is a cultural and social center for transplants from the Alentejo, the traditional southern province of Portugal (and historically the poorest region in the country). While the food is mainly hearty and simple, come for the ambience. It's a good place to try regional specialties such as pork with clams, or the super-sweet, eggy almond dessert called *charcada*. The full-bodied Alentejo red wine is cheap and solid (lunch specials, Tue-the food court, join the young, trendy, hungry, and thirsty crowd grazing among a wide variety of options. Assemble a sampling of local treats, and grab a seat at the big, shared tables in the middle. The north wall is a row of stalls run by big-name Lisbon chefs offering quality dishes at reasonable prices (enticing dinner plates for €10). And there are also branches of Honorato (a local "gourmet burger" chain), O Prego da Peixaria (fish and steak sandwiches), Sea Me (a Chiado institution for seafood—with their notorious "octopus hot dog"), Aloma (in the west outer aisle, for the best pastries), and Santini (the venerable Portuguese gelateria). Get wine and beer from separate stalls in the center. You may find affordable *percebes* (barnacles) at several seafood stalls. On the west side, an aisle just outside of the main hall is lined with wonderful seafood bars.

Restaurant and a View: Above the main entrance (south side) is a great viewpoint for a wide shot of the market din below, and the quality **$$$ Pap'Açôrda Restaurant,** a long-respected place for traditional Portuguese cuisine, with a top chef. They serve seasonal specials and a €20 three-course lunch special on weekdays (12:00-18:00) in a modern, spacious dining room with professional service and an inviting menu (daily Tue-Sun 12:00-24:00, closed Mon, +351 213 464 811).

Mercado de Campo de Ourique

A trendy marketplace fills this 19th-century iron-and-glass market. Compared to Mercado da Ribera, it's less crowded and more purely local. Produce stalls, fishmongers, and bakeries sell everything from pigs' ears to fragrant bunches of cilantro (most close in the evening). At lunch and dinner, local diners pick up meals from whichever counter appeals: pork, seafood, Japanese, wine, beer, coffee, meat, produce, artisanal gelato, and so on (most eateries open daily 10:00-23:00).

Getting There: It's a couple of miles west of Rossio. Take a taxi or Uber, or hop on trolley #28E and ride to the second-to-last stop (Igreja do Santo Condestável; market is behind the big church). Lisbon's most interesting cemetery is one stop farther, at the end of the trolley line.

Sun 12:00-15:00 & 19:00-22:00, Mon 19:00-22:00, slip into the closed-looking building at Rua das Portas de Santo Antão 58 and climb stairs to the right, +351 213 469 231). They host folk singing in the grand ballroom (often on Sat from 15:00) and ballroom dancing (on many Sun from 15:00 to 19:00), except in summer when it's too hot (mid-June-mid-Sept).

$ Casa do Alentejo Bar, in the same building, serves cheap bar food and wine, either in the sleek-and-trendy interior or out on the little patio (spicy meat dishes, hearty cheeses, other tapas; daily 12:00-23:00, to the right of the stairs, look for *taberna* sign on main floor).

$$$$ Restaurante Solar dos Presuntos keeps the theater crowd happily fed with meat and seafood specialties. Its upstairs is more elegant, while the downstairs—with a colorful, open kitchen—is higher energy. Photos of Lisbon's celebrities and politicians who eat here enliven the walls. This place can take advantage of its popularity and bulldoze tourists into spending a lot—order cautiously and know what you're paying for. Reservations are smart (big splittable portions, good wine list, see daily suggestions, Mon-Sat 12:00-15:30 & 19:00-23:00, closed Sun, at the top end of Rua das Portas de Santo Antão at #150, +351 213 424 253, www.solardospresuntos.com).

$ Cantinho São José is a wonderfully untouristy, cheap-and-cheery hole-in-the-wall a block beyond the main restaurant zone. Its extremely tight, tiled interior is jammed with tiny tables filled by big locals ordering hearty, splittable portions of Portuguese classics—for far less money than the tourist traps nearby (Sun-Fri 9:00-24:00, closed Sat, Rua São José 94, +351 213 427 866).

On or near Avenida da Liberdade

These spots are in a residential neighborhood, near my recommended accommodations (Avenida Metro stop). For locations, see the "Lisbon's Avenida da Liberdade" map on page 114.

$$$$ Cervejaria Ribadouro is a favorite splurge for locals for quality meat and shellfish (daily 12:00-24:00, Avenida da Liberdade 155 at intersection with Rua do Salitre, +351 213 549 411). Seafood prices are listed by weight—the waiter can help you determine the cost of a portion. For a fun, quick, €15 per-person meal, order a small draught beer *(uma imperial)*, 100 grams (about a quarter pound) of *percebes* (barnacles), and *pão torrado com manteiga* (toasted bread with butter).

$$$ Restaurante A Gina, glowing like a mirage in a vacant lot that used to be a theater zone, is a good dinner option. Cloth bibs embroidered with Gina's name help you appreciate the tasty traditional Portuguese grilled meat and fish with abandon. Gina and her staff scramble to give this wonderful place a genuine friendliness; the son, Rui, speaks English. It's two minutes off of Avenida da Liberdade (directly behind recommended Hotel Lisboa Plaza—look for signs, RS%—free dessert port with this book, daily 12:00-15:00 & 18:00-24:00, reservations recommended, +351 213 420 296).

$$ Quermesse Restaurante is a fun, bright, and creative place serving Mediterranean dishes with plenty of cod and friendly service. Half the seating is in an old-school grocery store—when

---

Appetizers Aren't Free

Remember: In Portugal, there's no such thing as a free munch. Appetizers brought to your table before you order (such as olives, bread, and fancy pâtés) are not free. This is not a tourist gimmick—it's a Portuguese tradition, meant to curb your hunger while looking at the menu and waiting for your main dish to arrive. So if you don't want to pay for them, just push them aside after the waiter brings them. Don't eat any of it—not even one olive—or you'll be charged (only €1-2 for the simpler appetizers, but it can be annoying if you don't expect it).

---

reserving, request "in the store" (daily 12:00-15:00 & 19:00-24:00, Rua da Glória 85, +351 211 507 901).

Near Praça Martim Moniz

For locations, see the "Lisbon Center Restaurants" map on page 118.

$$ Tentações de Goa, run by Maria and her chef-owner husband from Goa, is a sweet hole-in-the-wall with authentic Goan cuisine and ambience. It's buried deep in a tangle of lanes in the Mouraria district, a block uphill from Praça da Figueira (Mon-Sat 12:00-15:00 & 19:00-22:00, closed Sun, from Poço do Borratém follow a lane uphill to Rua de São Pedro Mártir 23, +351 218 875 824).

$$$ Cervejaria Ramiro—an old-school restaurant serving well-respected seafood and steak, is hugely popular and becoming quite touristy. It's a good choice if you like bustle and happy energy with great seafood. Arrive early or late to avoid a very long line (Tue-Sun 12:00-24:00, closed Mon, a couple of blocks north of Praça Martim Moniz at Avenida Almirante Reis 1H, +351 218 851 024).

Below the Cathedral

These places are at the southeast corner of the Baixa, on the way to the Alfama.

$ Nova Pombalina is a busy little joint that serves quick sandwiches, soups, and exotic fresh-squeezed juices. It's famous among office workers for its suckling pig sandwich *(sandes de leitão)*. They have good *piri-piri* sauce on request. From Praça do Comércio, it's five blocks toward the castle, on the corner of Rua do Comércio and Rua da Madalena (Mon-Sat 8:00-19:00, closed Sun, Rua do Comércio 2, +351 218 874 360).

$$ Mesa Kreol offers a lively taste of Portugal's former overseas colonies—with cuisine from Cape Verde, Mozambique, Angola, and Brazil. Its interior is small, cozy, and nondescript, but the cuisine is a bold and flavorful change of pace. Manager Ju enjoys helping his guests navigate the menu, and there's often live music (Tue-Sun 19:00-24:00, closed Mon, Arco das Portas do Mar 29—see map on next page, mobile +351 910 629 690).

THE ALFAMA

Lunch on Largo do Contador Mor: This leafy and picturesque square, just under the castle, has a few interchangeable **$$** restaurants serving up decent plates of grilled sardines *(sardinhas grelhadas)*. But the real star of the square is **$ Miss Can,** an engaging, colorful, and stylish little shop that's injecting some contemporary class into the beloved Portuguese tradition of canned fish. Three young, hip Lisboners have returned to their roots (their families have been in the sardine biz for generations) to create fresh new packaging for a variety of canned sardines, mackerel, and cod. Peruse their shop, and pick a can or two to eat with bread, salad, and a drink at one of their inviting little café tables (daily 11:00-19:00, at #17, mobile +351 910 007 004, www.miss-can.com).

Near the Santa Luzia Viewpoint: $$$ Farol de Santa Luzia, which offers a nice seafood feast with a delicate and delightful dining area, is a favorite of mine for dinner at the top of the Alfama. A family-run place with a local clientele, it offers the Algarve *cataplana* style of cooking—simmered in a copper pot (€27 big *cataplana* of meat, fish, or shellfish for two; indoor seating only, Mon-Sat 17:30-23:00, closed Sun, Largo Santa Luzia 5, across from Santa Luzia viewpoint terrace, tiny sign, +351 218 863 884; Andre, Luis, and family).

Near Largo Rodrigues de Freitas: For more of an adventure with your meal, walk past Largo das Portas do Sol and follow the trolley tracks along Rua de São Tomé to a square called Largo Rodrigues de Freitas—if riding trolley #12E, it's the first stop over the big hill. On this square, **$$ Restaurante Frei Papinhas** is a classic, family-run, hole-in-the-wall where you can feast on fresh seafood with the neighborhood crowd. Dine inside, or at rickety tables across the street in a charming square—where you can watch the trolleys rattle by (daily 12:00-16:00 & 19:00-24:00, Rua de São Tome 13, +351 218 866 471).

Fado Deep in the Alfama: While the Bairro Alto is far livelier at night and has a better energy, the Alfama still has a unique charm. My favorite places for dinner with fado are described earlier, under "Entertainment in Lisbon."

CHIADO

This neighborhood has some of Lisbon's trendiest restaurants. If you don't mind paying a bit more to experience the city's burgeoning food scene, venture up into these inviting streets. Remember that the more traditional Bairro Alto neighborhood—covered in

Alfama Restaurants

1 Mesa Kreol
2 Miss Can
3 Farol de Santa Luzia
4 Rest. Frei Papinhas

5 A Baiuca Rest. & Fado
6 Clube de Fado
7 Casa de Linhares Fado

the next section—is just a few minutes' walk away. For locations, see the "Lisbon Center Restaurants" map on page 118.

$$$ Restaurante Vicente, at the southern edge of Chiado, fills a former brick-arched coal warehouse with rustic-trendy decor and excellent Alentejo cuisine from Portugal's arid southern heartland. The hearty, delicious meals come with real history: Traditionally, coal cellars like this one came with a crow named "Vicente" to act as an early-warning system for polluted air—like the proverbial canary in a coal mine (Mon-Fri 12:30-15:30 & 19:30-24:00, Sat-Sun 19:30-24:00, Rua das Flores 6, +351 218-066-142).

$$ Carmo Restaurante and Bar offers delicious updated Portuguese cooking. You can share a few *petiscos* (Portuguese-style tapas), or get well-presented main courses. In good weather, sit out on the inviting square, under a leafy canopy. Otherwise, take advantage of the chic-but-homey setting, with a series of smaller rooms (weekday lunch deals, tempting desserts, daily 12:00-23:00, Largo do Carmo 11, +351 213 460 088).

$$$ Cervejaria da Trindade—a bright, boisterous, beer hall—is full of historic tiles, seafood, and tourists. While over-priced and in all the guidebooks, it's a historic landmark (see description on page 50). The seafood is charged by weight—clarify prices when you order (daily 12:00-24:00, liveliest 20:00-22:00, air-con, courtyard, a block down from São Roque Church at Rua Nova da Trindade 20C, +351 213 423 506).

$$$ Palácio Chiado took an abandoned, 18th-century private mansion and turned it into a luxurious but relaxed dining space with two bars and five differently themed restaurants, each occupying a palatial room. Feel like royalty as you ascend the grand staircase to chill with a hanging, winged lion (daily 12:00-24:00, Rua do Alecrim 70, +351 210 101 184).

$$$ By the Wine, a trendy yet accessible wine bar fills a cellar under a green-bottled vaulted ceiling. They serve a few dozen Portuguese wines by the glass, thoughtfully paired with local cold cuts and cheeses, small plates, and main dishes. It's less intimate and informative than Lisbon Winery (described later), but busier, more atmospheric, and more food-focused (Tue-Sun 12:00-24:00, Mon from 18:00, Rua das Flores 41, +351 213 420 319).

$$$ Café Buenos Aires is a friendly place serving Argentinian cuisine (lots of red meat), hearty dinner salads, vegetarian homemade pasta, and famous chocolate cake. Dine in the intimate woody interior, or at fun tables outside on a characteristic, stepped pedestrian lane with views across to the Alfama (daily 18:00-24:00, Rua do Duque 31, +351 213-420-739). Above this place and on the same lane is **$$ Solar do Duque,** a typical Portuguese eatery with romantic tables on the stepped lane (daily, Rua do Duque 67, +351 213 426 901).

$ El Rei D'Frango ("King of Chicken") is a local favorite for huge portions of affordable, stick-to-your-ribs grilled meat and fish specialties (but, strangely, not much chicken), served in an unpretentious little hole-in-the-wall. It's on the steep stepped lanes at the very bottom of Chiado, behind Rossio station (Mon-Sat 10:00-22:00, closed Sun, Calçada do Duque 5, +351 213 424 066).

$$$ Café no Chiado is a local favorite for its brief, accessible menu. Perched on an upper street overlooking the square in front of the São Carlos national theater, it has a casual-classy interior, and the outdoor tables—on a tiny square under red-and-black awnings—feel very European (daily 12:00-24:00, Largo do Picadeiro, +351 213 460 502).

Food Court Atop the Armazéns do Chiado Mall: The sixth-floor food court at this shopping center, between the Bairro Alto and the Baixa, hosts mostly fast-food and chain restaurants, but mixes in a few actual restaurants with castle views (daily 12:00-23:00, between Rua Garrett and Rua da Assunção; from the lower town, find the inconspicuous elevator at Rua do Crucifixo 89 or 113, next to the Baixa-Chiado Metro entrance). Among your many options are: **Loja das Sopas**, with hearty soups and cheap fixed-price meals; **Companhia das Sandes**, which offers up sandwiches and healthy, big-bowl pasta salads topped with tropical fruits; and **Restaurant Chimarrão**, serving Brazilian cuisine and an impressive *rodizio:* an all-you-can-eat buffet of salad, veggies, and endless beef, ham, pork, sausage, and chicken (€11 for weekday lunch, €13 for dinner and on weekends).

Heavenly Custard Tarts: $ Manteigaria is simply the best place in Lisbon's downtown for *pastel de nata*—everyone's favorite local pastry. They serve only this one treat, constantly churning out the lovable little €1 custard pies so you'll get them hot from the oven. While here, enjoy a look at the busy kitchen (daily until 24:00, Rua Loreto 2 just off Praça Luís de Camões).

José Avillez Restaurants in Chiado

One of Portugal's top celebrity chefs, José Avillez, has elevated and modernized Portuguese classics with international influences and techniques. He runs 16 restaurants and, judging by the energy in each and the local buzz, he's on a roll. While his **Belcanto** flagship restaurant boasts two Michelin stars (costly tasting menus, closed Sun-Mon, book well in advance, Largo de São Carlos 10, www.belcanto.pt), his other places are perfectly accessible. They have a common personality: trendy; high-energy; open kitchens; young, smart, English-speaking waitstaff; open daily (12:00-24:00); and, unless eating very early or very late, a reservation is smart. One call center works for all (+351 211 914 498) or book online (www.joseavillez.pt).

Bairro do Avillez Taberna and **Páteo** are two distinct and thriving places at the same address. **$$$ Taberna** is a casual place serving Portuguese classics as small plates and main courses. Its bar is a hit with well-dressed and mingling locals sharing plates family-style. **$$$$ Páteo,** in the back under a big skylight, is more formal and expensive, offering a full menu of fish and seafood, vegetarian dishes, and salads (Rua Nova da Trindade 18).

\$\$\$ Café Lisboa is a romantic and elegant bistro with tasty modern Portuguese dishes and great seating both indoors and out (in front of the opera house at Largo de São Carlos 23).

\$\$\$ Cantinho do Avillez has a casual vibe and a more international menu. Dining here, you'll feel like you're in on a Lisbon foodie secret (Rua dos Duques de Bragança 7).

\$\$\$ Pizzaria Lisboa simply serves top-quality pizza in a dressy yet fun setting (Rua dos Duques de Bragança 5).

\$ Pitaria, with a few stools at small tables, offers top-quality Middle-Eastern take-away and the best shawarma and falafel in town (Rua Nova da Trindade 11).

THE BAIRRO ALTO

For a characteristic meal in Old World surroundings, the Bairro Alto is hard to beat. For locations, see the "Lisbon Center Restaurants" map on page 118.

Fado with Dinner in Bairro Alto: For a most memorable dining experience with live fado music in the Bairro Alto, consider these two options: **Restaurante Adega do Ribatejo** (more casual, Rua Diario de Noticias 23), or **O Faia** (top-end splurge with quality food and fado, Rua da Barroca 54). Both are described earlier, under "Entertainment in Lisbon."

\$\$ Restaurante Bota Alta ("The High Boot") is a classic—if a bit touristy—little eatery with a timeless Portuguese ambience, tight seating, and reliably good food. Portions are big, and Paulo offers a fun dessert sampler plate. Reservations are smart (Mon-Sat 12:00-14:30 & 19:00-23:00, closed Sun, at corner of Travessa da Queimada and Rua da Atalaia, +351 213 427 959).

\$\$ A Primavera do Jerónimo is a quintessential Bairro Alto joint serving traditional home-style plates in a jam-packed, joyfully characteristic scene. Rafael and Helena love serving stuffed squid and Brás-style cod—whipped into a frittata with potatoes and onions (Mon-Sat opens at 19:30, closed off-season Sun; reserve, come early, or wait; at Travessa da Espera 38, a few steps below recommended fado place Canto do Camões, +351 213 420 477).

\$\$\$ Lisbon Winery, a modern little wine bar, has a passion for the best wines, cheeses, and meats. With quality local ingredients, cork walls, and fado music playing, it's a perfect storm of Portuguese culture. Their expert staff knows Portuguese wines and ports and how to complement them with tasty foods. Tell your server your budget, and they'll work within it (Tue-Sun 15:00-23:00, closed Mon, Rua da Barroca 13, +351 218 260 132, www.lisbonwinery.com). They also do wine tastings (€65/person, typically starts at 15:30 or 17:30 and lasts 2 hours).

Príncipe Real Garden Eateries
(Jardim do Príncipe Real)

This delightful parklike square is just a five-minute hike up Rua Dom Pedro V above the top of the Elevador da Glória funicular and the Bairro Alto. While this area is a shopping mecca (see "Shopping in Lisbon," earlier), it also has a lovely array of eateries. For locations, see the "Lisbon's Avenida da Liberdade" map on page 114.

The park itself has an unforgettable cedar tree shaped into a canopy over shady benches and a *quiosque* that doubles as a trendy, youthful wine and beer hangout. Also below the tree's canopy is **$$$ Esplanada do Príncipe Real,** with delightful seating—either at outdoor tables under shady branches or in the glassed-in interior. Skip the pricey, forgettable food—I'd just order a drink and savor the ambience (+351 210 965 699).

$$$ A Cevicheria is the neighborhood's big foodie draw, where (under a giant stuffed octopus) Chef Kiko serves elegant Peruvian/Portuguese dishes—specializing in flavorfully marinated raw fish and seafood ceviche. This deservedly popular place takes no reservations; arrive early or expect to wait (daily 12:00-24:00, a block toward Bairro Alto from the square at Rua Dom Pedro V 129, +351 218 038 815).

$$ Pavilhão Chines ("Chinese Pavilion"), a few doors down, is an eccentric, smoky, private museum-like bar with room after room slathered with an enormous collection of esoteric treasures. Come here to settle into a club chair and sip a drink rather than to eat (daily from 18:00, Rua Dom Pedro V 89, billiards in back).

Lisbon Connections

BY PLANE

Lisbon's easy-to-manage Portela Airport is five miles northeast of downtown (code: LIS; for airport info, see www.aeroportolisboa.pt or call +351 218 413 700 or +351 800 201 201).

Getting Between the Airport and Downtown

Getting to and from the airport is a snap. Figure on 20 to 30 minutes by taxi, Uber, or bus (depending on traffic) or 30 to 40 minutes by Metro.

By Taxi or Uber: Taxis line up on the curb at the airport, but are notoriously aggressive in gouging arriving travelers. You're more likely to get a fair price—and skip any line—by going upstairs to the departures curb and hopping into a cab as it drops off its riders. Better yet, request a ride using Uber. Either way, a ride to or from town should cost €10-15 to the center. If taking a taxi, insist on using the meter—it should start at around €4 and be set to *Tarifa 1* (or *Tarifa 2* for nights, weekends, and holidays). There is no "airport fee" supplement, but there is a legitimate €1.60 fee for your luggage (not per bag).

To return to the airport from downtown, use Uber or hail a cab on the street. Skip the outrageously overpriced "taxi vouchers" sold by the airport TI—these are for rides outside the center and more than double your cost.

If heading for a town other than Lisbon, talk with cabbies about a set "off-the-meter" fare. I recently negotiated a fast and efficient ride from the airport directly to Nazaré by taxi for around €100.

By Bus: While dirt-cheap public buses leave from the airport curb, they are not intended for people with luggage. The Aerobus shuttle is faster and nearly as cheap (€4, 3/hour, runs 8:00-21:00, departs outside arrival level at bus stop marked "Aerobus #1," www.aerobus.pt). Be sure to use Aerobus #1, which heads to the city center, with stops at Marquês de Pombal, Avenida da Liberdade, Restauradores, Rossio, Praça do Comércio, and Cais do Sodré. Route #2 avoids the downtown and ends in the financial district, but makes a handy stop at the bus station at Sete Rios if you plan to go elsewhere immediately (see "By Bus," later). Aerobus tickets are sold at the airport TI or at the bus stop for the same price, or you can buy them online in advance at a discount. (But for three passengers, a taxi or Uber is likely cheaper than this bus.)

By Metro: The Metro gets you into town affordably (for the price of a single transit ticket) and avoids traffic. But to reach central Lisbon, you'll have to change from the airport's suburb-focused red line to the green line (at Alameda)—it's time-consuming (figure 30-40 minutes total) and inconvenient if you're packing heavy. To find the Metro, exit the airport arrivals hall and turn right to find the Aeroporto stop. Before boarding, buy a reloadable Viva Viagem card and your choice of ticket (zapping, single-ride, or all-day) at the ticket machine (see details under "Getting Around Lisbon" on page 11).

BY TRAIN

All of Lisbon's train stations are connected to the Metro system, making departures and arrivals a breeze. For train info, call +351 808 208 208, visit www.cp.pt, or check Germany's excellent all-Europe website, www.bahn.com.

Santa Apolónia station covers international trains and nearly all of Portugal. Located just east of the Alfama, it has ATMs, a morning-only TI, baggage storage, a Pingo Doce supermarket, and good Metro and bus connections to the town center. A taxi or Uber from Santa Apolónia to any of my recommended hotels costs roughly €8. Bus #728, #759, #782, and #794 go to or near Praça do

Comércio, and bus #759 continues to Rossio and Praça dos Restauradores. To get to the bus stop from the station, look for the Metro sign, walk past the escalators to exit the station, and go right along busy Avenida Infante Dom Henrique to the bus stop.

Most trains using Santa Apolónia also stop at **Oriente** station, farther from the center, near Parque das Nações (M: Oriente; for more on this architecturally interesting station, see page 85).

Rossio station, which is in the town center and an easy walk from most recommended hotels, handles the most convenient trains to Sintra (direct, 2/hour, 40 minutes, buy tickets from machines at track level on second floor). It also has trains to Óbidos and Nazaré (but since both destinations require multiple transfers, the bus is a better option). The all-Portugal ticket office on the ground floor (next to Starbucks) sells long-distance and international train tickets (Mon-Fri 8:00-14:30 & 15:30-20:00, closed Sat-Sun, cash only).

Cais do Sodré station, near the waterfront just west of Praça do Comércio (M: Cais do Sodré), is the terminus for a short regional line that runs along the coast from Lisbon, making stops at Belém (10 minutes), Estoril (30 minutes), and Cascais (40 minutes).

Train Connections

Note: Most trains leaving from Santa Apolónia pass through Oriente station a few minutes later.

From Lisbon by Train to: Madrid (likely 1/day, "Lusitânia" night train, 11 hours, departs from Santa Apolónia station, arrives at Madrid's Chamartín station), **Évora** (4/day, 1.5 hours, departs Oriente), **Lagos** (3/day, 4 hours, departs Oriente, transfer in Tunes), **Tavira** (4/day, 4.5 hours, departs Oriente, change at Faro), **Coimbra** (almost hourly, 2 hours, departs Santa Apolónia),

Nazaré/Valado (5/day, 3-4 hours, transfer in Caldas da Rainha or Coimbra-B; bus is better—see next page), **Óbidos** (3/day, 2.5 hours, departs Santa Apolónia; also 7/day, 2.5 hours, transfer in Melecas or Cacém, departs Rossio), **Porto** (hourly, 3 hours, departs Oriente), **Sintra** (Mon-Fri 2/hour, Sat-Sun hourly, 40 minutes, departs Rossio; 6/hour, 45 minutes, departs Oriente).

To Salema: To reach Salema, you'll first need to get to **Lagos**, which is about 4 hours from Lisbon by train (see above) or bus (see next). Trains from Lisbon to the Algarve leave from Oriente station on the Lisboa-Faro line. At Tunes, a transfer to a local train takes you as far as Lagos. From there, it's a cheap bus ride or a pricier taxi ride to Salema.

BY BUS

Lisbon's efficient Sete Rios bus station is in the modern part of the city, three miles inland. It has ATMs, schedules, and two side-by-side information offices—one for buses within Portugal, the other for international routes (Rede Expressos, which sells tickets for routes—including to Spain—even if operated by other companies like Alsa). While it's possible to buy bus tickets up to a week in advance, you can almost always buy a ticket just a few minutes before departure. The EVA company covers the south of Portugal (www.eva-bus.com), while Rede Nacional de Expressos does the rest of the country (www.rede-expressos.pt; bus info for both companies—toll +351 707 223 344).

The bus station is across the street from the large Sete Rios train station, which sits above the Jardim Zoológico Metro stop. To get from the bus station to downtown Lisbon, it's a €6 taxi or Uber ride or a short Metro trip on the blue line (from bus station, walk down stairs and across to enter the Sete Rios train station, then follow signs for *Metro: Jardim Zoológico*).

From Lisbon by Bus to: Coimbra (hourly, 2.5 hours), **Nazaré** (6/day, 2 hours), **Fátima** (1-2/hour, 1.5 hours), **Batalha** (5/day, 2 hours), **Alcobaça** (7/day, 2 hours, some transfer in Caldas da Rainha), **Óbidos** (hourly, 1 hour, departs from near Campo Grande Metro stop), **Porto** (best via Rede Expressos, at least hourly, 3 hours), **Évora** (almost hourly, 1.5 hours), **Lagos** (hourly direct, 4 hours, easier than train, must book ahead, get details at TI), **Tavira** (5/day direct, 4 hours), **Madrid** (2-3/day, 9 hours, overnight option, www.avanzabus.com), **Sevilla** (4/day, 7 hours, overnight option, may be fewer off-season, run by Alsa, www.alsa.es).

BY CRUISE SHIP

Most cruise ships dock at one of three terminals: Jardim do Tabaco (immediately below the Alfama), Santa Apolónia (near the train station of the same name, just beyond the Alfama), or Alcântara (about two miles west of downtown, between the center and Belém).

The taxis that wait here are notoriously dishonest. You may be better off using Uber, walking a block or two away from the terminal and hailing a passing cab on the street (not at a taxi stand), or riding a cruise-line shuttle service to Praça da Figueira. Hop-on, hop-off bus tours, which conveniently link up major sights—stop at the cruise terminals (see "Tours in Lisbon" earlier in this chapter).

From **Alcântara,** you can hop on trolley #15E (use pedestrian underpass to reach trolley stop) or bus #728—either way, it's about a 15-minute ride. (Both of these also go—in the opposite direction—to the sights in Belém.)

Jardim do Tobaco and **Santa Apolónia** are close enough to walk to the Baixa (15-20 minutes)—just cross busy Avenida Infante Dom Henrique and walk along a row of houses with the river on your left) until you reach Praça do Comércio. Or you can take bus #728 from near either terminal to Praça do Comércio.

LISBON

SINTRA

For centuries, Portugal's aristocracy considered Sintra (SEEN-trah)—just 15 miles northwest of Lisbon—the perfect place to escape from city life. Now tourists do, too. Sintra is a mix of natural and man-made beauty: fantasy castles set amid exotic tropical plants, lush green valleys, and craggy hilltops with hazy views of the Atlantic and Lisbon. This was the summer getaway of Portugal's kings. Those with money and a desire to be close to royalty built their palaces amid luxuriant gardens in the same neighborhood. Lord Byron called this bundle of royal fancies and aristocratic dreams a "glorious Eden," and even though it's mobbed with tourists today, it's still magnificent.

With extra time, explore the rugged and picturesque westernmost tip of Portugal at Cabo da Roca.

PLANNING YOUR TIME

Sintra makes a great day trip from Lisbon. Here you can romp along the ruined ramparts of a deserted Moorish castle, and climb through the Versailles of Portugal—the Pena Palace—on a neighboring hilltop.

It's such an ideal side-trip, in fact, that Sintra can be mobbed (especially July through Sept). Saturdays and Sundays are popular with Portuguese, while foreign tourists clog the town on Mondays (when many Lisbon museums are closed, but all major Sintra sights are open). Crowds are a bit lighter on Tuesdays through Fridays. Sintra's complicated landscape—with lots of hills and one-way roads between the big sights—adds to the challenge. A trip here requires patience and a flexible schedule. For the most stress-free visit possible, consider this good one-day plan:

Near Lisbon

To
Coimbra
& Porto

A-8

A-9

A-1

N-9

Cabo
da
Roca

Sintra
N-247

PARQUE
DAS NAÇÕES

IC-19

Lisbon

2

Guincho
Beach
N-9

N-247

Estoril

A-5

Belém

4

3

1

VASCO DA
GAMA BRIDGE

Rio Tejo

A-12

Cascais

25TH OF APRIL
BRIDGE

Cacilhas

CRISTO
REI MON.

Barreiro

Pinhal
Novo

To
Évora

Costa da
Caparica

Atlantic Ocean

A-2

A-6

To Algarve
(by expressway)

Setúbal

IC-1

To Algarve
(by scenic
coastal route)

N-379

Portinho
da Arrábida

Cabo
Espichel

5 Km

5 Miles

SINTRA

<u>Major Train Stations</u>
1 Santa Apolónia
2 Oriente
3 Rossio
4 Cais do Sodré

Leave Lisbon around 8:30 to arrive in Sintra by 9:15 (most major sights open between 9:30 and 9:45—if you arrive much later, you'll be hopelessly mired in crowds all day). Pick up a map at the TI in Sintra's train station and catch bus #434 in front of the station to Pena Palace. Visit the palace, walk down to the Moorish Castle ruins, scramble over its ramparts, then hike about 45 minutes back down to town via Vila Sassetti (or take bus #434). Have lunch (unless you already had a picnic, or lunched at the Pena Palace's café), explore the town, and—if you're not exhausted yet—visit the National Palace (in town) or the Quinta da Regaleira (a 10-minute walk). Finally, catch the train back to Lisbon in time for dinner. This general plan also works well for drivers, who ideally should leave their car in Lisbon (or park upon arrival in Sintra) and use public transportation to get between the sights.

Spending the night in Sintra lets you get an early start or visit the sights later in the day (the Moorish Castle is even better at closing time, with the sun low in the sky)—and lets you savor the small town after dark, when it's quieter. Drivers in particular could consider overnighting in Sintra on the way to or from Lisbon.

GETTING TO SINTRA

Catch the **train** to Sintra from Lisbon's central Rossio station (direct, Mon-Fri 2/hour, Sat-Sun hourly, 40 minutes; also 6/hour from the less central Oriente station, 45 minutes). The trip is covered by the LisboaCard or the €10 version of Lisbon's all-day transit pass; if "zapping" with a Viva Viagem card, it's €1.90 each way (see page 12). Note that none of these passes work on local buses once you're in Sintra.

To avoid early-morning lines at the station in Lisbon, buy or charge up your card the night before (otherwise, buy it when you get to Rossio station—using the ticket machines or windows upstairs, at track level). During your ride, take in the views of the 18th-century aqueduct (on the left) and the workaday Lisbon suburbs. Relax...Sintra is at the end of the line.

Sintra is far easier by train than by **car** from Lisbon. Consider waiting until after you visit Sintra to pick up your rental car. If you do drive to Sintra, see "Route Tips" at the end of this chapter for advice.

Orientation to Sintra

Sintra is small. The town itself sprawls at the foot of a hill, an easy 10-minute walk (or quick bus ride) from the train station. The National Palace, with its unmistakable pair of cone-shaped chimneys, is in the center of the town, a block from the TI, and the Quinta da Regaleira is a 10-minute walk away. The other two main sights—Pena Palace and the Moorish Castle—hover on the hilltop above (you can see the castle's serrated wall on the hilltop). Most people take the bus up, but avid hikers enjoy the walk (figure an hour steeply uphill; see "Hiking Between Sintra and the Castles," later.)

TOURIST INFORMATION

Sintra has two TIs: a small one in the train station (daily 9:00-13:00 & 14:00-18:00, +351 211 932 545) and a larger one a block off the main square in the Museu Regional building (daily 9:00-18:00, Aug until 19:00, +351 219 231 157, www.visitlisboa.com). Pick up a free map with information on sights and a local Scotturb bus schedule. Hikers can download walking routes from the park administration website (www.parquesdesintra.pt).

ARRIVAL IN SINTRA

By Train: Upon arrival, stop at the TI in the station to get a map. To **bus** to the town center, hop on Scotturb #434 (exit the station to the right, buy €6.90 all-day ticket from street vendors or from the driver, schedules posted at stop; for more bus info, see "Getting Around Sintra," later). The bus stops in town first (near the National Palace) before heading up to the Moorish Castle and Pena Palace, then loops back down to the station and town.

You can also reach the town center easily on **foot** (exit the station and go left, then turn left when you hit the turreted town hall)—it's about a 10-minute walk along a mostly level road along the lip of a ravine. Along the way you'll see modern "art" and hippies selling handmade trinkets.

By Car: See "Route Tips" at the end of this chapter for tips including where to park.

HELPFUL HINTS

Festivals: The lively Festival de Sintra music and dance festival runs from late May to early July (www.festivaldesintra.pt).

Money: You'll find a few ATMs near the train station, another inside the main TI, and one on Rua das Padarias, just up the hill from the recommended Casa Piriquita.

WC: There's a free WC near the small, central parking lot where horse carriages wait (Calçada do Pelourinho).

Bring a Picnic: To save a few euros, consider bringing a picnic from Lisbon—restaurants here can be pricey, though there is a very basic grocery store (see "Eating in Sintra," later).

Local Guide: Cristina Quental works mainly in Lisbon, but lives near Sintra and can meet you at the station (€150/half-day, €240/day; mobile +351 919 922 480, anacristinaquental@ hotmail.com).

GETTING AROUND SINTRA

All forms of transportation use the same very congested, single-lane, one-way road that loops up the hill and passes the main monuments. That means that no way is faster than any other—maybe just a bit more comfortable. Note that the town center may be closed to traffic on busy weekends—confirm your stop with the driver.

By Bus: The best choice for most is Scotturb bus **#434,** which loops together all the important stops—the train station, the town center, the Moorish Castle ruins, and the Pena Palace—before

Sintra

← One-way streets
--- Bus #434

300 Meters
300 Yards

To N-247
Cabo
da Roca

To
Lisbon
& Pena Palace
via bus #434

C. AZENHAS

#434
& 435 B

CASA
MIRADOURO
HOTEL

CARVALHEIRO

CASA
DO VALLE
GUESTHOUSE

SOTO MAIOR

MACEIRA

See Central Sintra detail map

TOWN
HALL

TRAIN
STN.
&

C. CASTANHAIS

NATIONAL
PALACE

Main
Square

T

P

VOLTA DO DUCHE
(MAIN ROAD)

RUA MURTAS

#435 B

QUINTA DA
REGALEIRA

TOWN
CENTER

#434

P   Ravine

B

Liberdade
Park

To
Monserrate &
Cabo da Roca

AVENIDA GARRETT

#434
& 435 B

#435
B

ESTRADA DE PENA

R. SALDANHA

VILA
SASSETTI

R. CAMÕES

N-375

Santa Maria Way

SANTA
MARIA

R. DA TRINDADE

GREAT
VIEW!

TICKET
BOOTH

MOORISH
CASTLE

Steep
hill

TICKET
BOOTH

To
Train
Station

CALÇADA PENA

#434
B

Parking #1   P

ESTRADA DE PENA

B   #454

Pena Park

Parking #3

MAIN
ENTRANCE

Parking #2   P

LAGOS (LAKES)
ENTRANCE &
TICKET DESK

PENA
SHUTTLE
BUS

B   #434

PENA
PALACE

TICKET
BOOTH

To
High Cross

SINTRA

heading back to town and the train station (4/hour—subject to
traffic; €6.90 hop-on, hop-off ticket good all day; buy from driver
or street vendors at train station; first bus departs train station at
9:15; last bus leaves station at 19:50; entire circuit takes 30 minutes
without traffic).

A different bus, **#435,** goes from the train station to Quinta da
Regaleira and the Monserrate gardens (3/hour, single-ride ticket

priced by distance—about €2.50; €5 hop-on, hop-off ticket good all day; not covered by bus #434 ticket).

Crowd-Beating Tips: Busy days bring very long lines at popular bus stops, and buses crammed with people. If there's a long line at the train station bus stop, consider walking into town and catching the bus near the National Palace instead. When returning to town from the Pena Palace, consider walking about 10 minutes (mostly downhill) back along the road to the Moorish Castle bus stop, where there's usually no line. Scotturb's information office across from the train station is most crowded during morning hours.

By Tuk-Tuk: Noisy, bouncy, but fun tuk-tuks charge €5/person for a breezy ride from town or the station to the Moorish Castle, Pena Palace, or Quinta da Regaleira (you can also book tuk-tuks for a "guided tour" loop).

By Taxi: Figure €10 from the center up to any one of the sights.

By Carriage: Clip-clop horse carriages cost about €30 for 25 minutes. They can take you anywhere; you'll likely see them waiting on the little square near the bus stop just in front of the National Palace.

Sights in Sintra

Ticket Tips: For the Pena Palace, Moorish Castle, and National Palace, it's smart and simple to buy **single tickets online** a few days in advance at www.parquesdesintra.pt. Buying online will only save you about 5 percent, but it does save you a long, frustrating wait (usually 30 minutes or more) at ticket counters or ticket machines. **Combo-tickets** for these three sights offer similar cost savings but are not sold online. Unless you're going to all three sights, and didn't buy single tickets in advance, the combo deal is not worthwhile.

The **LisboaCard** gets you discounted entry at the Pena Palace, Moorish Castle, National Palace, and the Monserrate gardens (about 5 percent, only valid onsite). Be sure to bring the LisboaCard booklet, which contains coupons required for some of the discounts.

The Quinta da Regaleira is run by a private organization, so is not a part of any palace or castle combo-ticket.

ON THE HILL ABOVE SINTRA

These sights cap the hill high above Sintra—connected by bus #434. If walking between them, figure 10 minutes between the Pena Palace main entrance and the Moorish Castle, and another 10 minutes to the Pena Palace's lower "Lakes/Lagos" entrance. Be careful walking along the congested road, with its narrow shoulder and ankle-twisting cobbles.

▲▲Pena Palace (Palácio de Pena)

This magical hilltop palace sits high above Sintra, above the Moorish Castle ruins. In the 19th century, Portugal had a very romantic prince, the German-born Prince Ferdinand. A contemporary and cousin of Bavaria's "Mad" King Ludwig (of Disneyesque Neuschwanstein Castle fame), Ferdinand was also a cousin of England's Prince Albert (Queen Victoria's husband). Flamboyant Ferdinand hired a German architect to build a fantasy castle,

mixing elements of German and Portuguese style. He ended up with a crazy Neo-fortified casserole of Gothic towers, Renaissance domes, Moorish minarets, Manueline carvings, Disneyland playfulness, and an *azulejo* (tile) toilet for his wife.

Cost and Hours: Palace and gardens-€14, shuttle bus-€3 round-trip; May-mid-Sept palace open daily 9:30-18:30, gardens 9:00-19:00, shorter hours off-season; audioguide-€3, +351 219 105 340, www.parquesdesintra.pt.

Getting In: There are two entrances to the castle grounds: the lower "Lakes/Lagos" entrance (at the bottom of the park, across from the first parking lot you come to), and the main entrance (just below the castle itself). It's a 20-minute walk between these two (you'll pass the Moorish Castle ticket booth between them). While the lower entrance is less crowded, it's best to use the main entrance if possible, since it's closer to the castle.

At the main entrance, purchase your ticket at the small hut next to the gate (if there's a long line, look for ticket machines just downhill—toward the Moorish Castle).

To avoid the 10-minute uphill climb from the entrance to the palace (and enjoy a lift back down later), you could catch the green shuttle bus, which departs from straight ahead as you enter (buy with your palace ticket—or inside gift shop—but *not* from driver, departs about every 10 minutes). Lines for the shuttle bus can be longer than ticket lines. Before buying your palace ticket, take a look inside the main gate to see how many people are waiting in line for the shuttle, then decide if you want to add the shuttle ticket to your palace entry.

Be sure to pick up the *Parques e Palácios* map, with a helpful illustration of the castle on one side and a circular, 1.5-hour walking route of the park on the other.

SINTRA

Eating: The palace has an inexpensive **$** view café and a pricier **$$** restaurant. If you brought your lunch with you, enjoy it in the picnic-perfect gardens either before or after your visit—with views fit for a king.

◆ Self-Guided Tour: The palace, built in the mid- to late-1800s, is so well-preserved that it feels as if it's the day after the royal family fled Portugal in 1910 (during a popular revolt that eventually made way for today's modern republic). This gives the place an intimacy rarely seen in palaces.

• *After you hop off the green shuttle bus, hike up the ramp and go through the Moorish archway with alligator decor. Cross the drawbridge that*

doesn't draw and join a slack-jawed world of tourists frozen in deep knee-bends with their cameras cocked.

Palace Interior: Show your ticket again to enter the palace itself. Inside, at the base of the stairs, you'll see a bust of King Ferdinand II, who built this castle from 1840 until his death in 1885. Though German, he was a romantic proponent of his adopted culture and did much to preserve Portugal's architectural and artistic heritage.

• *Next you'll pop out into the...*

Courtyard: The palace was built on the site of a 16th-century monastery; the courtyard was the former location of the cloister. In spite of its plushness, the palace retains the monkish coziness of several small rooms gathered in two levels around the cloister.

Like its big brother in Belém, the monastery housed followers of St. Jerome, the hermit monk. Like their namesake, the monks wanted to be isolated, and this was about as isolated as you could be around here 500 years ago. The spot was also a popular pilgrimage destination for its statue of "Our Lady of the Feathers" (*pena* means feather—hence the palace's name). In 1498 King Manuel was up here enjoying the view when he spied Vasco da Gama sailing up the river, returning safely from his great voyage. To celebrate and give thanks, the king turned what was a humble wooden monastery into a fine stone palace.

• *From here, follow the one-way route counterclockwise around the courtyard, dipping into a variety of rooms. These are especially worthy of attention.*

Dining Room and Pantry: Stuck into a cozy corner, the monastery's original refectory was decked out with the royal family's finest tableware and ceiling tiles.

Atelier (Workshop) of King Carlos I: King Carlos was a talented artist and a great patron of the arts. He often found refuge in painting—specifically in the latest style, Art Nouveau. Unfinished paintings and sketches eerily predict the king's unfinished rule.

King's Bedroom and Bathroom: The king enjoyed cutting-edge comforts, including a shower/tub imported from England, and even a telephone to listen to the opera when he couldn't face the Lisbon commute. The bedroom is decorated in classic Romantic style—dark, heavy, and crowded with knickknacks.

• *Now head upstairs (gripping the funky dragon-like handrail). Circling around the courtyard, you'll enter the wing called the Piano Nobile ("noble floor"). Go through a few daintily decorated rooms that belonged to ladies-in-waiting, and then enter the...*

Queen's Bedroom and Dressing Room: Study the melancholy photos of Queen Amelia (Amélie of Orléans), King Carlos, and their family in this room. The early 1900s were a rocky time for Portugal's royal family. The king and his eldest son were assassinated in 1908. His youngest son, Manuel II, became king until he, his mother the queen, and other members of the royal family fled Portugal during the 1910 revolution.

As you shuffle through the palace, you'll see state-of-the-art conveniences—such as the first flush toilets and hot shower in Portugal, and even a telephone room. The whole place is lovingly cluttered, typical of the Victorian horror of empty spaces.

• *At the end of this floor, step out onto the...*

Queen's Terrace: Enjoy a sweeping view from Lisbon to the mouth of the Rio Tejo. Find the Cristo Rei statue and the 25th of April Bridge. The statue on the distant ridge honors the palace's architect.

• *Heading back inside, you'll pass through some smaller rooms, then enter...*

The New Wing: This spacious addition to the original series of rooms around the cloister includes the apartments of the last king, the smoking room (with a tiled ceiling), and the fantastically furnished Great Hall.

On your way down the spiral staircase, take a detour to see the **Stag Room**—with well-antlered walls and a dramatic dome supported by a stout, palm-tree-like column. From here, you'll head down to see the abundant kitchen.

Just after, a view café conveniently welcomes us peasants. While many people take this as a sign to leave, we haven't yet seen some of the most scenic parts of the castle.

• *From the café, turn left and walk alongside the palace, then duck through one of the two huge, ornamental gateways on your left (the second one has a scowling Triton overhead). You'll emerge into the...*

Inner Patio: Take the stairs up to the pointed dome covered in green and white tiles (in front of the tallest red tower). This was the royal family's sumptuous private **chapel,** decorated in a variety of styles. The structure is Manueline, reminiscent of the Monastery of Jerónimos in Belém.

• *Heading back down into the patio, don't miss the little door under the chapel marked...*

The Wall Walk: If you aren't afraid of heights, follow this for a rampart ramble with great views—of the onion-domed balustrade, of the palace itself, and of the surrounding countryside—including the Moorish Castle on an adjacent hilltop. When the entire circuit is open, you'll circle all the way around the outside of the palace, and wind up back at the entrance. Otherwise, walk back the way you came.

• *From here, you can return directly to the main entrance (walk 10 minutes or catch the green shuttle bus), or detour for a self-guided tour of the park.*

Pena Palace Park: The lush, captivating, and sprawling palace grounds—rated ▲—are dotted with romantic surprises and provide a refreshing break from Sintra's crowds. Several landmarks within the park are signposted near the shuttle bus stop. Highlights include the High Cross (highest point around, with commanding views), chapels, a temple, giant sequoia trees, and exotic plants. To walk through the park after you tour the palace, take a 40-minute stroll downhill (following the map that came with your palace entry)—past greenhouses, pavilions, and a series of five manmade lakes—to the lower park gate, at the Lakes/Lagos entry, where you'll find a bus stop and the Estrada de Pena loop road. From here, it's a ten-minute hike uphill to the Moorish Castle, or a 20-minute hike back to the Pena Palace's main entrance.

▲Moorish Castle (Castelo dos Mouros)

Sintra's thousand-year-old ruins of a Moorish castle are lost in an enchanted forest and alive with winds of the past. They're a castle

lover's dream come true, and a great place for a picnic with a panoramic Atlantic view. Though built by the Moors, the castle was taken by Christian forces in 1147. It's one of the most classically perfect castles you'll find anywhere, with two hills

capped by hardy forts, connected by a crenellated wall walkway. (It's so idealized because it was significantly restored in the 19th century.)

Cost and Hours: €8, daily 9:00-18:30, +351 219 237 300, www.parquesdesintra.pt.

Getting In: From the main ticket booth (just uphill from the bus stop) to the castle entrance, it's an atmospheric 10-minute up-and-down stroll through a forested canyon, passing a few small exhibits and information plaques. If the main ticket booth is crowded, bypass it and simply continue to the castle itself, where there's another ticket booth that rarely has a wait. Either way, be sure to pick up the well-illustrated map, which has lots of insightful information.

Visiting the Castle: You'll enter the castle in a terraced area with a cafeteria, shop, and WCs, all sitting on top of a cistern. The castle walls and towers climb hills on either side of you. Do a hardy counterclockwise hike, conquering the lower one first, then heading up to the higher one. (Or, if you're tired, just walk up the central staircase to enjoy a breathtaking view.)

For the full experience, from where you entered, go right and take the stony stairs up to the keep. From the top tower, you can see how the wall twists and turns—following the contours of the land—as it connects over to the taller hilltop tower. Follow the crenellated path, with delirious views over Sintra down below and as far as the Atlantic. You'll go down, then back up the other side, ascending higher and higher to the top of the Royal Tower. From the summit, you enjoy great views across to Pena Palace, perched on its adjacent hilltop. From this pinnacle, you can gingerly descend to the cafeteria and entrance—having conquered the castle.

Hiking Between Sintra and the Castles

It's a steep one-hour hike from town up to the Moorish Castle and Pena Palace—challenging even for hardy hikers. But hiking back down to town after your hilltop visits (rather than cramming into an overstuffed bus) is an appealing 45-minute possibility for those with strong knees. Be sure to equip yourself with the TI's invaluable *Pedestrian Route* map—and get their advice—before you set out (maps may also be available at Moorish Castle or Pena Palace ticket offices).

The best route is to take a terraced path directly below the Moorish Castle, which leads past the **Vila Sassetti.** You'll find the trailhead at the end of the parking lot directly across from the Lakes/Lagos lower entrance of the Pena Palace grounds, and you'll also find a trail connecting to it near the Moorish Castle main ticket booth (near the bus stop). From here, the trail curls around the bottom of the Moorish Castle's rocky perch, then enters the grounds of the Vila Sassetti (open daily 10:00-18:00, until 17:00 off-season). Designed by theater set decorator Luigi Manini (who also did the Quinta da Regaleira, described later), the Vila Sassetti looks like an old Roman house with a terra cotta roof. You'll hike down to the villa itself, then traipse through its lower gardens into Sintra. (If the Villa is closed, you can also drop down—on steep steps—to footpaths that run through the woods above the main road.)

Yet another option is to walk down on the **"Santa Maria Way,"** which forks off in the opposite direction from the Moorish Castle entrance. However, this trail is mostly through thick woods and less scenic.

SINTRA

IN TOWN
These sights are all within easy walking distance of the town center.

▲National Palace (Palácio Nacional)
While the palace dates back to Moorish times, most of what you'll see is from the 15th-century reign of King João I, with later

Manueline architectural ornamentation from the 16th century. This oldest surviving royal palace in Portugal is still used for official receptions. Having housed royalty for 500 years (until 1910), it's fragrant with history.

Cost and Hours: €10, daily 9:30-18:30, audioguide-€3; look for white, double-coned building in town center—a 10-minute walk from the train station; +351 219 237 300, www.parquesdesintra.pt.

Tours: Free English tours depart the entrance at 14:30. The audioguide is informative, but as dry as an Alentejo summer.

❍ Self-Guided Tour: The palace is a one-way romp with little information provided. If touring on your own, read the brief descriptions in each room, and tune into the following notable parts of the palace.

• *Show your ticket, then head upstairs into the...*

Swan Room: This first room is the palace's banquet room. A king's daughter—who loved swans—married into a royal house in Belgium. The king missed the princess so much that he decorated the ceiling with her favorite animal.

Central Patio: This was a fortified medieval palace, so rather than having fancy gardens outside, it has a stay-awhile courtyard within its protective walls. Notice the unique chimneys. They provide powerful suction that removes the smoke from the kitchen and also creates a marvelous open-domed feeling (as you'll see at the end of your tour).

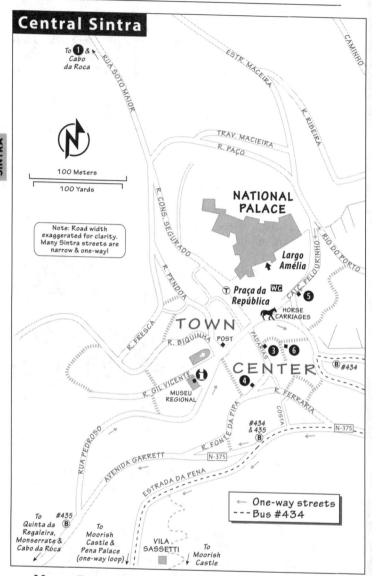

Central Sintra

Magpie Room: The queen caught King João I being a little too friendly with a lady-in-waiting. Frustrated by his court—abuzz with gossip—João had this ceiling painted with magpies. But to defend his honor, he illustrated each magpie quoting the king's slogan—*Por bem,* "For good." The 15th-century Moorish tiles are from Spain, brought in before the development of the famous, ubiquitous Portuguese tiles, and are considered some of the finest Moorish-Spanish tiles in all of Iberia.

SINTRA

Accommodations
1. To Casa Miradouro & Casa Do Valle Guesthouse
2. Monte Da Lua Guesthouse

Eateries
3. Casa Piriquita
4. Piriquita II Café & Binhoteca Wine Bar
5. Café da Villa
6. Mercearia do Beco Grocery
7. Rest. Regional de Sintra
8. InComum & Apeadeiro Rest.

Bedchamber of King Sebastian (Dom Sebastião): The king portrayed on the wall (to the right of where you enter) is King Sebastian, a gung-ho, medieval-type monarch who went to battle in Africa, following the Moors even after they were chased out of Europe. He disappeared in 1578 at age 24 (although he was almost certainly killed in Morocco, "Sebastianists" awaited his mythical return into the 19th century). With the king missing, Portugal was left in unstable times with only Sebastian's great uncle (King Henrique) as heir. The new king died within two years, and the throne passed to his great uncle, King Philip II of Spain, leading to 60 years of Spanish rule (1580-1640).

Note the ebony, silver, and painted copper headboard of the Italian Renaissance bed. The tiles in this room are considered the first Portuguese tiles—from the time of Manuel I. The corn-on-the-cob motif topping the tilework is a reminder of American discoveries.

More Main-Floor Rooms: From here, you'll walk through the **Julius Caesar Room,** with a Flemish tapestry of the Roman general-turned-ruler; the **Goddess Diana Courtyard;** and up the stairs to the **Galleon Room,** whose ceiling is painted with ships flying the flags of the great nautical powers of the day. Step out onto the balcony for views of a forested hillside scattered with the villas of aristocrats—and capped by the serrated wall of the Moorish Castle. Then, head up the stairs to walk through some smaller, simpler apartments with a few original furnishings.

• *Finally, you step into the glorious...*

Blazons Hall (a.k.a. Coat of Arms Room): The most striking room in the palace—under a golden dome and slathered in blue tiles—honors Portugal's loyal nobility. Study the richly decorated ceiling. The king's coat of arms at the top is surrounded by the coats of arms of his children; below that is a ring of stags; and just below, "supporting" the king are the coats of arms of Portugal's noble families. The Latin phrase circling the room reads, "Honoring all the noble families who've been loyal to the king." The 18th-century tiles hang from the walls like tapestries and show more stag hunting scenes. Enjoy the view: a garden-like countryside dotted with mansions of nobility who clamored to be near their king, the hill-capping castle,

and the wide-open Atlantic. You're in the westernmost room of the westernmost palace on the European continent.

• *Continue through the upper halls, peeking into the...*

Bedchamber and Prison of Alfonso VI: This king suffered from a fever as a child that left him mentally unstable. After he became king, he was removed by his wife and his brother—who became King Pedro II, locked him in this room for the rest of his life, and married his queen.

Yet More Rooms: As you continue, you'll pass through the **Chinese Room** (with an exquisite ivory-and-bone model of a Chinese pagoda). Downstairs, you can step out onto a private balcony and peer down into the **Palatine Chapel,** with a Mudejar wood-carved ceiling. Then you'll pass through a room of coffers (literal treasure chests) and head downstairs to the **Arab Room**—decorated with Moorish tiles, and with a little fountain in the middle; this was the preferred bedroom of João I. From here, you'll walk through a fancy **guest room** and into the **kitchen.** With all the latest in cooking technology, the palace chef could roast an entire cow on the spit, keep the king's plates warm in the iron dish warmer (with drawers below for the charcoal), and get really dizzy by looking up and spinning around three times.

On your way out, as you step back into the big entry hall, be sure to detour left into the **Manueline Room,** with carved-stone ropes over the doors and a grand chandelier, and a handy WC in the corner. You'll walk back through the Central Patio (peek into the blue-tiled **Grotto of the Baths** in the corner) and head for the exit. On your way out, watch for the easy-to-miss door on the right that lets you explore the manicured, terraced **gardens** surrounding the palace. Sit with a carved lion and enjoy views from one palace to another.

SOUTHWEST OF THE CENTER

These two sights line up on a road southwest of central Sintra. You can walk to Quinta da Regaleira, but Monserrate is quite a bit farther. Bus #435 stops at each one (see details earlier, under "Getting Around Sintra"), or you can take a tuk-tuk or taxi.

▲▲Quinta da Regaleira

This Neo-Everything (Manueline/Gothic/Renaissance) 1912 mansion and garden has mystical and Masonic twists. It was de-

signed by Italian opera-set designer Luigi Manini for a wealthy but disgruntled monarchist two years after the royal family was deposed. While the mansion—prickly with spires—is striking from the outside, its interior is nothing compared to the Pena Palace or National Palace. But the grounds are an utter delight to wander, with fanciful follies, secret underground passages, and lush landscaping. Many travelers (especially younger ones) find romping around these grounds more enjoyable than shuffling around the crowded interiors of the more famous palaces. Ask a local to pronounce "Regaleira" for you, and just try to repeat it.

Cost and Hours: €10, daily 10:00-18:30, closes earlier off-season, last entry one hour before closing, 10-minute walk from downtown Sintra, café, +351 219 106 650, www.regaleira.pt.

Tours: Excellent two-hour English tours fill up, so book ahead online or by phone (€15, includes entry, about hourly April-Sept, fewer off-season). The tour focuses on the garden, and can be longish unless you're into quirky Masonic esoterica.

Visiting the Quinta: As you enter, be sure to pick up the superb illustrated map of both the house and the gardens.

The **mansion** itself is striking—as it was designed to be. (In fact, that was its sole purpose.) You'll enter through the finest space, the Hunting Room, with an outrageously carved fireplace. From here you can explore three floors, filled mostly with well-presented exhibits on the design and construction of the place, and biographical sketches of the aristocrat and the architect who brought it to life. At the top floor, find the tight spiral stone staircase up to the view terrace.

The real highlight is the playful **gardens,** which stretch uphill from the mansion. Work your way up, past the elaborate private chapel, then to higher and higher crenellated viewpoints. Follow *Waterfall* signs to reach a refreshing artificial canyon with ponds and a cascade. Stepping stones lead across the main pond to the grottos that hide beneath, giving you a unique perspective. From the top of the waterfall, continue up to the "Portal of the Guardians"; inside, secret tunnels lead to the dramatic, spiral-staircase-wrapped well—burrowed 90 feet down into the hillside, and, like the rest of Quinta da Regaleira, more about showing off than about being functional. From here, more tunnels lead to other parts of the property; use your map to explore to your heart's content.

Monserrate

About 2.5 miles outside of Sintra—on the road past the Quinta da Regaleira—are the wonderful gardens of Monserrate. If you like tropical plants and exotic landscaping, a visit is time well-spent, though many find that the gardens at Pena Palace or the Quinta da Regaleira are just as good as these more famous grounds.

Cost and Hours: €8, palace open daily 9:30-18:30, park 9:00-19:00, +351 219 237 300, www.parquesdesintra.pt.

WEST OF SINTRA, ON THE COAST
Cabo da Roca

Wind-beaten, tourist-infested Cabo da Roca (KAH-boo dah ROH-kah) is the westernmost point in Europe, perhaps the inspiration for the Portuguese poet Luís de Camões' line, *"Onde a terra se acaba e o mar começa"* ("Where land ends and the sea begins"). It has a little shop, a café, and a tiny TI that sells an expensive "proof of being here" certificate. Take a photo instead. Nearby, on the road south to Cascais, you'll pass a good beach for wind, waves, sand, and the chance to be the last person in Europe to see the sun set. For a remote beach, drive to Praia Adraga (north of Cabo da Roca).

Sleeping in Sintra

Sintra works well as an overnight—allowing you to beat the crowds by tackling the sights early or late, and have the charming town to yourself after hours. To reach the first two places, head into town, turn right to pass in front of the National Palace, then continue steeply downhill on the road past Hotel Tivoli; they face each other at the very bottom of the street (free street parking, steep 10-minute hike back up to the town center). The final listing—cheaper and handier for train travelers—is directly across the street from the train station.

$$$ Casa Miradouro is a beautifully restored mansion from 1893, now run by Belgian expat Charlotte Lambregts. The creaky old house feels like a homey, upscale British B&B, with eight spacious, stylish rooms, an elegant lounge, castle and sea views, and a wonderful garden (good breakfast extra, Rua Sotto Major 55, mobile +351 914 292 203, www.casa-miradouro.com, mail@casa-miradouro.com).

$$$ Casa Do Valle Guesthouse offers 11 comfortable, modern rooms on several levels in a peaceful hillside location. They have a lovely garden and large deck with valley and castle views, a swimming pool, and a shared kitchen (extra for continental breakfast in your room, reception open until 18:30, behind Casa Miradouro at Rua da Paderna 5, +351 219 244 699, www.casadovalle.com, info@casadovalle.com).

$ Monte Da Lua Guesthouse has seven clean, simple rooms with shiny hardwood floors; some rooms face the train station, while others face a quieter ravine in the back (cheaper rooms with shared bath, no breakfast, Avenida Dr. Miguel Bombarda 51, +351 210 129 659, montedalua51@gmail.com).

Eating in Sintra

These listings are in the town of Sintra. To eat at the hilltop sights, there are cafés at both Pena Palace and the Moorish Palace, or you can pack a picnic.

LIGHT MEALS

Most of these (except Café da Villa) are on or near Rua das Padarias, the touristy little cobbled lane across the street from the National Palace. The sit-down restaurants in this zone are very pricey and touristy, but these are handy for a light, quick meal.

$ Casa Piriquita bills itself as "the" *antiga fabrica de queijadas*—historic maker of tiny, tasty tarts with a cheesy filling. It's good for a sweet and a coffee or a simple lunch, such as toasted sandwiches. Take a seat in the café (up a few steps) to avoid groups who rush in for pastries to go, or do battle and grab a half-dozen for about €5 (Tue-Thu 8:30-22:00, closed Wed, Rua das Padarias 1, +351 219 230 626).

$ Piriquita II, sister to Casa Piriquita, is a block farther up the lane and may have less commotion. It has a more extensive menu and a view terrace (Wed-Mon 8:30-20:00, closed Tue, Rua das Padarias 18, +351 219 230 626).

$$ Binhoteca, a welcoming little *enoteca,* provides wine lovers with an astonishing array of Portuguese wines and ports available by the glass (starting at €5), along with tasty meat-and-cheese plates, sandwiches, and salads. The knowledgeable staff is happy to explain what you're enjoying. It's a fun experience, but prices can add up (daily 10:00-19:00—and often later, Rua das Padarias 16, +351 219 230 444).

$$ Café da Villa, a favorite of bus drivers and tour guides, offers generous portions of homemade-style soups and salads in a homey pub-like setting. It's good for a quiet, inexpensive lunch, with a variety of fixed-price meal options (daily 12:00-24:00, facing the little bus-stop square in front of the National Palace at Calçada do Pelourinho 2, +351 219 241 174).

Groceries: Mercearia do Beco, just a few steps off Rua das Padarias, is a basic grocery store where you can assemble a picnic (daily 9:00-20:00, Rua Arco do Teixeira 17).

DINING

While there are plenty of tourist eateries in Sintra's old center, for a serious meal I'd head a couple of blocks away to the station area.

$$ Restaurante Regional de Sintra, which feeds locals and tourists very well, is my favorite place for dinner in Sintra. Gentle Paulo speaks English and serves huge, splittable portions (Tue-Thu 12:00-16:00 & 19:00-22:30, closed Wed, tucked to the right of the turreted town hall at Travessa do Municipio 2, +351 219 234 444).

$$$ InComum is working hard to bring a modern sensibility to traditional Portuguese cooking. The owners, who lived in Switzerland, pride themselves on serving Portuguese-inspired dishes with updated, international flair. The minimalist dining room is especially popular at lunchtime, when the weekday lunch special offers an affordable taste of their cooking (Sun-Fri 12:00-24:00, Sat from 16:30, Rua Dr. Alfredo Coasta 22, +351 219 243 719).

$$ Apeadeiro Restaurante, named for the platform along the track at the train station just a block away, is a quality eatery serving good food at good prices. Their daily specials can be split, allowing two to eat affordably (Fri-Wed 11:30-23:00, closed Thu, Avenida Dr. Miguel Bombarda 3, +351 219 231 804).

Sintra Connections

SINTRA

From Sintra by Train and Bus to: Lisbon (Mon-Fri 2 trains/hour to Rossio station, Sat-Sun hourly, 40 minutes; 6 trains/hour to Oriente station, 45 minutes), **Cascais** (bus #403 via Cabo da Roca, 45-60 minutes, 1-2/hour; express bus #417, 30 minutes, hourly; both buses fewer on weekends, catch either one at the Sintra train station).

ROUTE TIPS
Sintra Day Trip from Lisbon by Car

Cars are the curse of Sintra—all traffic, from cars to buses to tuk-tuks, has to nudge through town on a two-lane road, and parking is difficult (especially up at the hilltop castles).

If you insist on taking a car to Sintra, take the IC-19/A-37 freeway out of Lisbon (allow 30 minutes, not counting traffic delays). When you arrive in Sintra, follow *Centro Histórico* signs. It's smartest to simply **park your car** and use bus #434 to get around. The road into town (Volta do Duche) has some pay-and-display parking (4-hour maximum). And there's free parking on the road just behind the train station.

If you anticipate crowds, park in the (relatively) large lot down in the ravine between the train station and the TI. As you come into town, watch for the colorful, turreted Town Hall building on your right; take the tiny lane immediately after that building (the *no entry* signs are just for campers) and head down to the lot next to the Museu Anjos Teixeira. Climb up the stairs next to the museum, and you're on the main road into town.

It's tempting to drive up the **Moorish Castle** and **Pena Palace,** but be warned that parking up top is very limited (often jammed by about 10:00). The road makes a very long, one-way loop with no backtracking, so if you don't find a space you'll have to complete the loop and return back to the center. But if you want to take your chances, here's the plan: Head up the road with every other car and bus in town. You'll twist up, up, up on a dozen switchbacks. Approaching the sights, there are three marked parking lots (one by the lower Lakes/Lagos entrance to Pena Palace; another just before the main entrance to Pena Palace—this is probably your most convenient choice, if it has space; and a third one, just past the main entrance to Pena Palace). Monitors along the road suggest which lots might have space, and which are *completo*. All along the congested, cobbled road are a few well-marked roadside spaces. It's best to park as soon as you find something—anything—and then walk the rest of the way to connect the sights.

It's possible to make a **70-mile circular trip** and drive to all the destinations near Lisbon within a day (Lisbon–Belém–Sintra–Cabo da Roca–Cascais–Lisbon), but traffic congestion around Sintra, especially on weekends and during rush hour, can slow you down.

Loop Trip by Public Transportation

If you're bent on seeing sights west of Lisbon—Sintra, Cabo da Roca, and Cascais)—in a single long day, it can be done using public transportation. Start at the Sintra train station and buy a day pass good for all routes of the Scotturb **bus** (€15.10). Use the pass to take bus #434 to Sintra's sights, then go to Cabo da Roca on bus #403. When you're ready, catch the next bus #403 for the jaunt to Cascais and a seafood dinner on the waterfront (for more on Cascais, see page 91). To head from Sintra straight to Cascais—without the Cabo da Roca detour—take the faster bus #417.

From Cascais, returning to Lisbon is a snap—just buy a one-way **train** ticket to Lisbon at the train station (or use your Zapping card). You'll get off at the last stop on the line (Cais de Sodré Station), a five-minute walk from Praça do Comércio in downtown Lisbon. Or, to return to Sintra, hop on bus #417.

PRACTICALITIES

This section covers just the basics on traveling in Portugal (for more comprehensive information, see the latest edition of *Rick Steves Portugal*). You'll find free advice on specific topics at RickSteves.com/tips.

MONEY

Portugal uses the euro currency: 1 euro (€) = about $1.20. To convert prices in euros to dollars, add about 20 percent: €20 = about $24, €50 = about $60. (Check www.oanda.com for the latest exchange rates.)

To get cash, use a debit card to withdraw euros from an ATM; US debit cards with a Visa or MasterCard logo will work in any European ATM. In Portugal, look for *Multibanco* signs marked with a blue-and-white *MB* logo and, when possible, withdraw cash from these bank-run ATMs (maximum €200). Avoid "independent" ATMs, such as Travelex, Euronet, Moneybox, Your Cash, Cardpoint, and Cashzone. These have high fees and can be less secure.

Before departing, call your bank or credit-card company: Confirm that your card(s) will work overseas, ask about international transaction fees, and alert them that you'll be making withdrawals in Europe. Also ask for the PIN number for your credit card—you may need it for Europe's "chip-and-PIN" payment machines. Allow time for your bank to mail your PIN to you.

European cards use chip-and-PIN technology; most chip cards issued in the US instead require a signature. European card readers may generate a receipt for you to sign—or prompt you to enter your PIN (so it's good to know it). US credit cards may not work at some self-service payment machines (transit-ticket kiosks, parking kiosks, etc.). If your card won't work, look for a cashier who can process the transaction manually—or pay in cash.

"Tap to pay" cards and smartphone payment apps work in Europe just as they do in the US and sidestep chip-and-PIN compatibility issues.

To keep your cash, cards, and valuables safe, wear a money belt.

Dynamic Currency Conversion: If merchants offer to convert your purchase price into dollars (called dynamic currency conversion, or DCC), refuse this "service." You'll pay extra for the expensive convenience of seeing your charge in dollars. If an ATM offers to "lock in" or "guarantee" your conversion rate, choose "proceed without conversion." Other prompts might state, "You can be charged in dollars: Press YES for dollars, NO for euros." Always choose the local currency.

STAYING CONNECTED

The simplest solution is to bring your own device—mobile phone, tablet, or laptop—and use it just as you would at home (following the money-saving tips below). For more on phoning, see RickSteves.com/phoning. For a one-hour talk covering tech issues for travelers, see RickSteves.com/mobile-travel-skills.

To Call from a US Phone: Phone numbers in this book are presented exactly as you would dial them from a US mobile phone. For international access, press and hold the 0 key until you get a + sign, then dial the country code (351 for Portugal) and phone number. To dial from a US landline, replace + with 011 (US/Canada international access code).

From a European Landline: Replace + with 00 (Europe international access code), then dial the country code (351 for Portugal) and phone number.

Within Portugal: To place a domestic call (from a Portuguese landline or mobile), drop the +351 and dial the phone number.

Tips: If you bring your mobile phone, consider signing up for an international plan; most providers offer a simple bundle that includes calling, messaging, and data.

Use Wi-Fi whenever possible. Most hotels and many cafés offer free Wi-Fi, and you may also find it at tourist information offices (TIs), major museums, and public-transit hubs. With Wi-Fi you can use your phone or tablet to make free or low-cost calls via a calling app such as Skype, WhatsApp, FaceTime, or Google Hangouts. When you need to get online but can't find Wi-Fi, turn on your cellular network (or turn off airplane mode) just long enough for the task at hand.

Most **hotels** charge a fee for placing calls—ask for the rates before you dial. You can use a prepaid international phone card (*cartão telefónico com código pessoal,* usually available at newsstands, tobacco shops, and train stations) to call out from your hotel.

Sleep Code

Hotels in this book are categorized according to the average price of a standard double room with breakfast in high season.

$$$$	**Splurge:** Most rooms over €150
$$$	**Pricier:** €100-150
$$	**Moderate:** €70-100
$	**Budget:** €40-70
¢	**Backpacker:** Under €40
RS%	**Rick Steves discount**

Unless otherwise noted, credit cards are accepted, hotel staff speak basic English, and free Wi-Fi is available. Comparison-shop by checking prices at several hotels (on each hotel's own website, on a booking site, or by email). For the best deal, *book directly with the hotel.* Ask for a discount if paying in cash; if the listing includes **RS%,** request a Rick Steves discount.

SLEEPING

I've categorized my recommended accommodations based on price, indicated with a dollar-sign rating (see sidebar). In addition to standard hotels, I also list several simple, family-run hotels (listed as a *pensão* or *residencial*) and rooms in private homes *(quartos)* as budget alternatives. Portugal also has luxurious, government-sponsored historic inns *(pousadas),* which are full of Old World character but pricey.

Book your accommodations as soon as your itinerary is set, especially if you want to stay at one of my top listings or if you'll be traveling during busy times. You can do this by checking hotel websites and booking sites such as Hotels.com or Booking.com.

After you've zeroed in on your choice, book directly with the hotel itself. This increases the chances that the hotelier will be able to accommodate special needs or requests (such as shifting your reservation). When you book by phone or email, the owner avoids the commission paid to booking sites, giving them wiggle room to offer you a discount, a nicer room, or a free breakfast (if it's not already included).

For complicated requests, send an email with the following information: number and type of rooms; number of nights; arrival date; departure date; any special requests; and applicable discounts (such as a Rick Steves discount, cash discount, or promotional rate). Use the European style for writing dates: day/month/year.

In general, hotel prices can soften if you do any of the following: offer to pay cash, stay at least three nights, or travel off-season.

Room rates are especially volatile at larger hotels that use "dynamic pricing" to set rates. Prices can skyrocket during festivals and conventions, while business hotels can have deep discounts on weekends when demand plummets. Of the many hotels I recommend, it's difficult to say which will be the best value on a given day.

To find an apartment or room in a private home, try Airbnb, FlipKey, Booking.com, and the HomeAway family of sites (HomeAway, VRBO, and VacationRentals).

EATING

I've categorized my recommended eateries based on the average price of a typical main course, indicated with a dollar-sign rating (see sidebar). The Portuguese meal schedule is slightly later than in the US. Their breakfast *(pequeno almoço)* is often just coffee and a sweet roll. Lunch *(almoço)* is served between 12:30 and 14:00, while supper *(jantar)* is from about 19:30 to 21:30. All restaurants are smoke-free.

Eat fresh seafood in Portugal, except on Monday, when the fish isn't fresh. Cod *(bacalhau)* is a mainstay, but definitely an acquired taste. Fish soup (sopa de peixe) and shellfish soup *(sopa de mariscos)* are worth seeking out. Or, for a seafood blowout, look for cataplana (a feast from the sea, simmered in a copper pot). The "Portuguese paella" is *arroz de mariscos,* seafood stew with rice. *Carne de porco á Alentejana* is an interesting combination of pork and clams. *Caldo verde* is vegetable soup. *Frango assado* is roast chicken; ask for *piri-piri* sauce if you like it hot and spicy.

At a restaurant, be warned that if the waiter brings you an appetizer you didn't order (such as olives, bread, or pâtés), it isn't free. If you don't want it, push it to the side or ask the server to take it back—you won't be charged for what you don't touch. Eating just one olive means you pay for the whole dish.

Many restaurants save their customers money by portioning their dishes for two people. Menus often list prices for entrées in two columns: *dose* and *meia dose.* A *dose* (DOH-zeh) is generally enough to feed two, while a *meia dose* is a half-portion (plenty for one person). Restaurants have absolutely no problem with diners splitting a single dose. *Prato do dia* is the daily special.

When you want the bill, say, *"A conta, por favor."*

Tipping: In nearly all restaurants, service is included—your menu typically will indicate this by noting *serviço incluído.* Still, if you are pleased with the service, it's customary to leave up to 5 percent, or 10 percent for top-notch service or in a fancy place. Leave the tip on the table. It's best to tip in cash, even if you pay with your credit card (there's generally not a place to include a tip on a credit card slip). There's no need to tip if you order food at a counter.

Restaurant Price Code

Eateries in this book are categorized according to the average cost of a typical main course. Drinks, desserts, and splurge items can raise the price considerably.

$$$$	**Splurge:** Most main courses over €17
$$$	**Pricier:** €12-17
$$	**Moderate:** €7-12
$	**Budget:** Under €7

In Portugal, takeout food is **$**; a basic sit-down eatery is **$$**; a casual but more upscale restaurant is **$$$**; and a swanky splurge is **$$$$**.

TRANSPORTATION

By Bus and Train: Portugal straggles behind the rest of Europe in train service, but offers excellent bus transportation. Because of this, a Eurail Portugal Pass doesn't make much sense. The best public transportation option is to mix bus and train travel. Portugal has several bus companies, sometimes running buses to the same destinations and using the same transfer points. If you have to transfer, make sure to look for a bus with the same name/logo as the company you bought the ticket from. The largest national company is Rede Expressos (covers buses both north and south of Lisbon, www.rede-expressos.pt).

To research train schedules, see Portugal's train website (www.cp.pt, includes Spain and France connections) or Germany's excellent all-Europe website (www.bahn.com). For information on rail passes, visit RickSteves.com/rail.

By Car: It's cheaper to arrange most car rentals from the US. For tips on your insurance options, see RickSteves.com/cdw. Bring your driver's license. If you're starting your trip in big-city Lisbon, don't rent a car until you're on your way out (and consider renting from the airport location). Note that it's simpler to day-trip to Sintra by train rather than by car.

Superhighways come with tolls but save huge amounts of time if you're crossing the country (see www.portugaltolls.com). For some toll roads, you pick up a ticket as you enter. Other roads are tolled electronically using cameras, which identify cars by their license plate and charge the appropriate fees via a simple electronic payment system. To save some hassle paying tolls, rent a **Via Verde automated toll sensor** along with your car. Ask your car-rental agency about this toll system.

When you park, be sure your valuables are out of sight and locked in the trunk, or even better, with you or in your hotel room. Local road etiquette is similar to that in the US. Ask your rental company about the rules of the road, or check the US State Department website (www.travel.state.gov, search for Portugal in the "Learn About Your Destination" box, then select "Travel and Transportation").

HELPFUL HINTS

Travel Advisories: For updated health and safety conditions, including any restrictions for your destination, consult the US State Department's international travel website (www.travel.state.gov).

Emergency and Medical Help: For any emergency service—ambulance, police, or fire—call 112 from a mobile phone or landline (operators typically speak English). If you get sick, do as the Portuguese do and go to a pharmacist for advice. Or ask at your hotel for help—they'll know the nearest medical and emergency services.

For **passport problems,** contact the **US Embassy** (Lisbon—appointment required, dial +351 217 273 300, https://pt.usembassy.gov) or the **Canadian Embassy** (Lisbon—dial +351 213 164 600, consular services available Mon-Fri 9:00-12:00, www.canadaintenational.gc.ca/portugal).

ETIAS Registration: Beginning in late 2021, US and Canadian citizens may be required to register online with the European Travel Information and Authorization System (ETIAS) before entering certain European countries (quick and easy process, $8 fee, valid 3 years, www.etiasvisa.com).

Theft or Loss: Thieves target tourists throughout Portugal, especially in Lisbon and Porto. While hotel rooms are generally safe, thieves snatch purses, pick pockets, and break into cars. Be on guard, especially on the Metro and trolleys, and treat any disturbance around you as a smoke screen for theft. Enjoy the sightseeing, but be aware of your surroundings—wear your money belt.

To replace a passport, you'll need to go in person to an embassy (see above). Cancel and replace your credit and debit cards by calling these 24-hour US numbers with a mobile phone: Visa (dial +1-303-967-1096), MasterCard (dial +1-636-722-7111), and American Express (dial +1-336-393-1111). From a landline, you can call these US numbers collect by going through a local operator.

File a police report either on the spot or within a day or two; you'll need it to submit an insurance claim for lost or stolen rail passes or travel gear, and it can help with replacing your passport or credit and debit cards. For more information, see RickSteves.com/help.

Time: Portugal uses the 24-hour clock. It's the same through 12:00 noon, then keep going: 13:00, 14:00, and so on. Portugal, like most of continental Europe, is six/nine hours ahead of the East/West Coasts of the US.

Business Hours: Some businesses in Portugal take a lunch break (usually 12:00-13:30 or 12:30-14:00). Larger shops and museums stay open all day. Banks are generally open Monday through Friday from 8:30 to 15:00. Small shops are often open on Saturday only in the morning and are closed all day Sunday.

Dress Code: At churches, a modest dress code (no bare shoulders or shorts) is encouraged.

Holidays and Festivals: Europe celebrates many holidays, which can close sights and attract crowds (book hotel rooms ahead). For information on holidays and festivals in Portugal, check the country's website: www.visitportugal.com. For a simple list showing major—though not all—events, see RickSteves.com/festivals.

Numbers and Stumblers: What Americans call the second floor of a building is the first floor in Europe. Europeans write dates as day/month/year, so Christmas 2022 is 25/12/22. Commas are decimal points and vice versa—a dollar and a half is 1,50, and there are 5.280 feet in a mile. Portugal uses the metric system: A kilogram is 2.2 pounds; a liter is about a quart; and a kilometer is six-tenths of a mile.

RESOURCES FROM RICK STEVES

This Snapshot guide, excerpted from the latest edition of *Rick Steves Portugal,* is one of many titles in my series of guidebooks on European travel. I also produce a public television series, *Rick Steves' Europe,* and a public radio show, *Travel with Rick Steves.* My free online video library, Rick Steves Classroom Europe, offers a searchable database of short video clips on European history, culture, and geography (Classroom.RickSteves.com). My website, RickSteves.com, offers free travel information, a forum for travelers' comments, guidebook updates, my travel blog, an online travel store, and information on European rail passes and our tours of Europe. If you're bringing a mobile device, you can download my free Rick Steves Audio Europe app that features podcasts of my radio shows, my free Lisbon City Walk audio tour, and travel interviews about Portugal. For more information, see RickSteves.com/audioeurope. You can also follow me on Facebook, Twitter, and Instagram.

ADDITIONAL RESOURCES

Tourist Information: www.visitlisboa.com, www.visitportugal.com
Passports and Red Tape: www.travel.state.gov
Packing List: www.ricksteves.com/packing
Cheap Flights: www.kayak.com, www.google.com/flights
Airplane Carry-on Restrictions: www.tsa.gov
Updates for This Book: www.ricksteves.com/update

HOW WAS YOUR TRIP?

To share your tips, concerns, and discoveries after using this book, please fill out the survey at RickSteves.com/feedback. Thanks in advance—it helps a lot.

Portuguese Survival Phrases

In the phonetics, nasalized vowels are indicated by an n̲ or w̲. As you say the vowel, let its sound come through your nose as well as your mouth.

English	Portuguese	Pronunciation
Good day.	*Bom dia.*	bohn **dee**-ah
Do you speak English?	*Fala inglês?*	**fah**-lah een-**glaysh**
Yes. / No.	*Sim. / Não.*	seeng / now̲
I (don't) understand.	*(Não) compreendo.*	(now̲) kohn̲-pree-**ayn**-doo
Please.	*Por favor.*	poor fah-**vor**
Thank you. (said by male)	*Obrigado.*	oo-bree-**gah**-doo
Thank you. (said by female)	*Obrigada.*	oo-bree-**gah**-dah
I'm sorry.	*Desculpe.*	dish-**kool**-peh
Excuse me (to pass).	*Com licença.*	kohn̲ li-**sehn**-sah
(No) problem.	*(Não) há problema.*	(now̲) ah proo-**blay**-mah
Good.	*Bom.*	bohn̲
Goodbye.	*Adeus. / Ciao.*	ah-**deh**-oosh / chow
one / two	*um / dois*	oon̲ / doysh
three / four	*três / quatro*	traysh / **kwah**-troo
five / six	*cinco / seis*	**seeng**-koo / saysh
seven / eight	*sete / oito*	**seh**-teh / **oy**-too
nine / ten	*nove / dez*	**naw**-veh / dehsh
How much is it?	*Quanto é?*	**kwahn**-too eh
Write it?	*Escreva?*	ish-**kray**-vah
Is it free?	*É gratis?*	eh **grah**-teesh
Is it included?	*Está incluido?*	ish-**tah** een-kloo-**ee**-doo
Where can I find / buy...?	*Onde posso encontrar / comprar...?*	**ohn**-deh **paw**-soo ayn-kohn̲-**trar** / kohn̲-**prar**
I'd like / We'd like...	*Gostaria / Gostaríamos...*	goosh-tah-**ree**-ah / goosh-tah-**ree**-ah-moosh
...a room.	*...um quarto.*	oon̲ **kwar**-too
...a ticket to ___.	*...um bilhete para ___.*	oon̲ beel-**yeh**-teh **pah**-rah ___
Is it possible?	*É possível?*	eh poo-**see**-vehl
Where is...?	*Onde é que é...?*	**ohn**-deh eh keh eh
...the train station	*...a estação de comboio*	ah ish-tah-**sow̲** deh kohn̲-**boy**-yoo
...the bus station	*...a terminal de autocarros*	ah tehr-mee-**nahl** deh ow-too-**kah**-roosh
...the tourist information office	*...a posto de turismo*	ah **poh**-stoo deh too-**reez**-moo
...the toilet	*...a casa de banho*	ah **kah**-zah deh **bahn**-yoo
men	*homens*	**aw**-mayn̲sh
women	*mulheres*	mool-**yeh**-rish
left / right	*esquerda / direita*	ish-**kehr**-dah / dee-**ray**-tah
straight	*em frente*	ayn̲ **frayn**-teh
What time does this open / close?	*As que horas é que abre / fecha?*	ahsh keh **aw**-rahsh eh keh **ah**-breh / **feh**-shah
At what time?	*As que horas?*	ahsh keh **aw**-rahsh
Just a moment.	*Um momento.*	oon̲ moo-**mayn**-too
now / soon / later	*agora / em breve / mais tarde*	ah-**goh**-rah / ayn̲ **bray**-veh / maish **tar**-deh
today / tomorrow	*hoje / amanhã*	**oh**-zheh / ah-ming-**yah**

PRACTICALITIES

In a Portuguese Restaurant

English	Portuguese	Pronunciation
I'd like / We'd like...	Gostaria / Gostaríamos...	goosh-tah-**ree**-ah / goosh-tah-**ree**-ah-moosh
...to reserve...	...de reservar...	deh reh-zehr-**var**
...a table for one. / two.	...uma mesa para uma. / duas.	**oo**-mah **may**-zah **pah**-rah **oo**-mah / **doo**-ahsh
Non-smoking.	Não fumar.	no<u>w</u> foo-**mar**
Is this table free?	Esta mesa está livre?	**ehsh**-tah **meh**-zah ish-**tah lee**-vreh
The menu (in English), please.	A ementa (em inglês) por favor.	ah eh-**mayn**-tah (ay<u>n</u> een-**glaysh**) poor fah-vor
service (not) included	serviço (não) incluído	sehr-**vee**-soo (no<u>w</u>) een-kloo-**ee**-doo
cover charge	coberto	koh-**behr**-too
to go	para fora	**pah**-rah **foh**-rah
with / without	com / sem	koh<u>n</u> / say<u>n</u>
and / or	e / ou	ee / oh
specialty of the house	especialidade da casa	ish-peh-see-ah-lee-**dah**-deh dah **kah**-zah
half portion	meia dose	**may**-ah **doh**-zeh
daily special	prato do dia	**prah**-too doo **dee**-ah
tourist menu	ementa turística	eh-**mayn**-tah too-**reesh**-tee-kah
appetizers	entradas	ay<u>n</u>-**trah**-dahsh
bread / cheese	pão / queijo	pow / **kay**-zhoo
sandwich	sandes	**sahn**-desh
soup / salad	sopa / salada	**soh**-pah / sah-**lah**-dah
meat	carne	**kar**-neh
poultry	aves	**ah**-vish
fish / seafood	peixe / marisco	**pay**-shee / mah-**reesh**-koo
fruit	fruta	**froo**-tah
vegetables	legumes	lay-**goo**-mish
dessert	sobremesa	soo-breh-**may**-zah
tap water	água da torneira	**ah**-gwah dah tor-**nay**-rah
mineral water	água mineral	**ah**-gwah mee-neh-**rahl**
milk	leite	**lay**-teh
(orange) juice	sumo (de laranja)	**soo**-moo (deh lah-**rah<u>n</u>**-zhah)
coffee / tea	café / chá	kah-**feh** / shah
wine	vinho	**veen**-yoo
red / white	tinto / branco	**teen**-too / **brang**-koo
glass / bottle	copo / garrafa	**koh**-poo / gah-**rah**-fah
beer	cerveja	sehr-**vay**-zhah
Cheers!	Saúde!	sah-**oo**-deh
More. / Another.	Mais. / Outro.	maish / **oh**-troo
The same.	O mesmo.	oo **mehsh**-moo
The bill, please.	A conta, por favor.	ah-**kohn**-tah poor fah-**vor**
tip	gorjeta	gor-**zheh**-tah
Delicious!	Delicioso!	deh-lee-see-**oh**-zoo

For many more pages of survival phrases for your trip to Portugal, check out *Rick Steves Portuguese Phrase Book*.

INDEX

Explore Europe

At ricksteves.com you can browse through thousands of articles, videos, photos and radio interviews, plus find a wealth of money-saving travel tips for planning your dream trip. And with our mobile-friendly website, you can easily access all this great travel information anywhere you go.

TV Shows

Preview the places you'll visit by watching entire half-hour episodes of *Rick Steves' Europe* (choose from all 100 shows) on-demand, for free.

your travel dreams into affordable reality

Radio Interviews

Enjoy ready access to Rick's vast library of radio interviews covering travel tips and cultural insights that relate specifically to your Europe travel plans.

Travel Forums

Learn, ask, share! Our online community of savvy travelers is a great resource for first-time travelers to Europe, as well as seasoned pros.

Travel News

Subscribe to our free Travel News e-newsletter, and get monthly updates from Rick on what's happening in Europe.

Classroom Europe

Check out our free resource for educators with 400+ short video clips from the *Rick Steves' Europe* TV show.

Rick's Free Travel App

Get your FREE **Rick Steves Audio Europe**™ app to enjoy…

- Dozens of self-guided tours of Europe's top museums, sights and historic walks

- Hundreds of tracks filled with cultural insights and sightseeing tips from Rick's radio interviews

- All organized into handy geographic playlists

- For Apple and Android

With Rick whispering in your ear, Europe gets even better.

Find out more at ricksteves.com

Gear up for your next adventure at ricksteves.com

Light Luggage

Pack light and right with Rick Steves' affordable, custom-designed rolling carry-on bags, backpacks, day packs and shoulder bags.

Accessories

From packing cubes to moneybelts and beyond, Rick has personally selected the travel goodies that will help your trip go smoother.

Save time and energy

This guidebook is your independent-travel toolkit. But for all it delivers, it's still up to you to devote the time and energy it takes to manage the preparation and logistics that are essential for a happy trip. If that's a hassle, there's a solution.

Rick Steves Tours

A Rick Steves tour takes you to Europe's most interesting places with great

with minimum stress

guides and small groups. We follow Rick's favorite itineraries, ride in comfy buses, stay in family-run hotels, and bring you intimately close to the Europe you've traveled so far to see. Most importantly, we take away the logistical headaches so you can focus on the fun.

Join the fun

This year we'll take thousands of free-spirited travelers—nearly half of them repeat customers— along with us on 50 different itineraries, from Athens to Istanbul. Is a Rick Steves tour the right fit for your travel dreams?

Find out at ricksteves.com, where you can also check seat availability and sign up. Europe is best experienced with happy travel partners. We hope you can join us.

See our itineraries at ricksteves.com

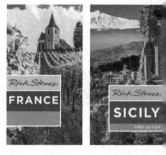

BEST OF GUIDES

Full-color guides in an easy-to-scan format. Focused on top sights and experiences in the most popular European destinations

Best of England
Best of Europe
Best of France
Best of Germany
Best of Ireland
Best of Italy
Best of Scotland
Best of Spain

COMPREHENSIVE GUIDES

City, country, and regional guides printed on Bible-thin paper. Packed with detailed coverage for a multi-week trip exploring iconic sights and venturing off the beaten path

Amsterdam & the Netherlands
Barcelona
Belgium: Bruges, Brussels, Antwerp & Ghent
Berlin
Budapest
Croatia & Slovenia
Eastern Europe
England
Florence & Tuscany
France
Germany
Great Britain
Greece: Athens & the Peloponnese
Iceland
Ireland
Istanbul
Italy
London
Paris
Portugal
Prague & the Czech Republic
Provence & the French Riviera
Rome
Scandinavia
Scotland
Sicily
Spain
Switzerland
Venice
Vienna, Salzburg & Tirol

E BEST OF ROME

taly's capital, is studded with
remnants and floodlit fountain
From the Vatican to the Colos-
th crazy traffic in between, Rome
rful, huge, and exhausting. The
he heat, and the weighty history

of the Eternal City where Caesars walked
can make tourists wilt. Recharge by taking siestas, gelato breaks, and after-dark
walks, strolling from one atmospheric
square to another in the refreshing evening air.

ntheon—which
me until the
000 years old
er 1,500.)

hens in the Vat-
the humanistic

tators fought
r, entertaining

Rick Steves books are available from your favorite bookseller.
Many guides are available as ebooks.

POCKET GUIDES

Compact color guides for shorter trips

SNAPSHOT GUIDES

Focused single-destination coverage

CRUISE PORTS GUIDES

Reference for cruise ports of call

Complete your library with...

TRAVEL SKILLS & CULTURE

Study up on travel skills and gain insight on history and culture

PHRASE BOOKS & DICTIONARIES

PLANNING MAPS

Photo Credits

Avalon Travel
Hachette Book Group
1700 Fourth Street
Berkeley, CA 94710

Printed in Canada by Friesens.
Fifth Edition. First printing April 2021.

ISBN 978-1-64171-382-5

For the latest on Rick's talks, guidebooks, tours, public television series, and public radio show, contact Rick Steves' Europe, 130 Fourth Avenue North, Edmonds, WA 98020, 425/771-8303, www.ricksteves.com, rick@ricksteves.com.

Rick Steves' Europe
Managing Editor: Jennifer Madison Davis
Assistant Managing Editor: Cathy Lu
Editors: Glenn Eriksen, Suzanne Kotz, Rosie Leutzinger, Jessica Shaw, Carrie Shepherd
Editorial & Production Assistant: Megan Simms
Researcher: Robert Wright
Research Assistance: Rich Earl, Lisa Friend
Contributor: Gene Openshaw
Graphic Content Director: Sandra Hundacker
Maps & Graphics: David C. Hoerlein, Lauren Mills, Mary Rostad
Digital Asset Coordinator: Orin Dubrow

Avalon Travel
Senior Editor and Series Manager: Madhu Prasher
Associate Managing Editors: Jamie Andrade, Sierra Machado
Indexer: Stephen Callahan
Production & Typesetting: Lisi Baldwin, Jane Musser
Cover Design: Kimberly Glyder Design
Maps & Graphics: Kat Bennett, Mike Morgenfeld

Let's Keep on Travelin'

Your trip doesn't need to end.

Follow Rick on social media!

KEEP ON TRAVELIN'
Rick Steves